PREPARING
for
Your Marriage

William J. McRae

ZONDERVAN
PUBLISHING HOUSE OF THE ZONDERVAN CORPORATION
GRAND RAPIDS, MICHIGAN 49506

PREPARING FOR YOUR MARRIAGE
Copyright © 1980 by The Zondervan Corporation
Grand Rapids, Michigan

Third printing 1982

Library of Congress Cataloging in Publication Data

McRae, William J
    Preparing for your marriage.
        1. Marriage counseling.   2.   Family—Religious
life.   I. Title.
HQ10.M353   362.8'286   80-22317
ISBN 0-310-42761-4

Unless otherwise indicated, Scripture quotations are from the *New American Standard Bible* © 1972 by The Lockman Foundation, Creation House, Carol Stream, Illinois.

Printed in the United States of America

To
Mary Lynn
Elisabeth
Janice
Mark

Contents

Part Three: Before Your Marriage

Part Four: Your Wedding and After

Foreword

All marriages are happy; it's the living together afterward that causes all the trouble! As marital plans are made a couple plans where they will live, how they will decorate, and how they will pay for where they will live, but very few couples plan *how* to live together. In this premarital manual Bill McRae sets forth a thoroughly biblical, practical plan for "the living-together process" of marriage.

In a day when there are more plans for living apart than living together this book is a fresh breeze. For the premarital counselors and counselees who are looking for more than a polite discussion of the wedding ceremony you have opened the right book.

Tim Timmons
Maximum Life Communications, Inc.

Acknowledgments

Without the active participation of dozens of couples in our premarriage counseling program over the past eight years, this study guide would never have become a reality. I am most grateful to each one for their willingness to be part of an experiment. Their helpful evaluations have been invaluable.

Special recognition is offered to Mike and Penny Eizenga, who worked with me in the final revisions of the manuscript, offering many practical and helpful insights from the perspective of an engaged couple.

I wish to thank the elders of Believers Chapel, Dallas, Texas, and North Park Community Chapel, London, Ontario, for their constant encouragement and for the freedom they have granted me to develop this program with their congregations.

The art work has been done by Mrs. Catherine Goodmurphy. Mrs. Glenda Martin has typed and retyped the manuscript which Mrs. Mary Lou Sheeler has read and edited. To each one I am deeply indebted.

Genuine appreciation is publicly expressed to my wife, Marilyn, for the immense investments she has made in both our marriage and this manuscript.

How Do I Love Thee?

How do I love thee? Let me count the ways.
I love thee to the depth and breadth and height
My soul can reach, when feeling out of sight
For the ends of Being and ideal Grace.
I love thee to the level of every day's
Most quiet need, by sun and candlelight
I love thee purely, as they turn from praise.
I love thee freely, as men strive for right;
I love thee with passion put to use
In my old griefs, and with my childhood's faith
I love thee with a love I seemed to lose
With my lost saints—I love thee with the breath,
Smiles, tears, of all my life!—and, if God choose,
I shall but love thee better after death.

—Elizabeth Barrett Browning

Introduction

There is little or no happiness in ninety percent of American homes!

This is the considered opinion of a nationally known psychiatrist.

Almost 50 percent of our marriages end in the tragedy of divorce, and over 75 percent of all teen-age marriages terminate in the courtroom. An undetermined number of young people are so disillusioned with marriage that it is no longer even a desirable option for them, and for many, marriage is really nothing more than an "armed truce." What once was holy wedlock has become in the words of Oscar Faust nothing but an "unholy deadlock." If the amount of time evangelical pastors spend in marriage counseling is any indication, marriage is a major problem even among Christians and in evangelical churches. What are the reasons? Is there an answer?

Personal experience and careful observation have led me to a conclusion that is neither profound nor original. However, it has become such a deep personal conviction that it has shaped a major part of my ministry.

Simply stated, I feel that most couples enter into marriage unprepared. Their expectations are unrealistic, their roles are undeveloped, their responsibilities are unknown, and their goals are undetermined. They are naive and immature, and are without sufficient direction and dedication. They undertake the colossal task of erecting a thirty-to forty-year relationship without the proper tools or adequate foundation.

This conviction, however, does not stand alone. In addition, I take marriage to be an extremely solemn commitment. From the depth of my being I urge a young couple not to enter into marriage "lightly, but rather with due consideration, solemnity, and godly fear." Coupled with this is an awesome sense of personal responsibility associated with officiating at a wedding. How can one pronounce a couple husband and wife without feeling some responsibility for the product?

Eight years ago these convictions led to the decision that the couples I would marry must be willing to participate in a premarriage study program.

The material that has been developed and used over these years is essentially the content of this book. It has been an adventure in preventative ministry. The testimonies of the "graduates" have encouraged me to make it available to a wider circle of couples. It is written with the prayer that our gracious and glorious Lord will use it to cultivate a host of marriages that will both mirror His relationship with His heavenly Bride and yield the choicest fruits to be enjoyed on earth.

The Objectives

1. To guide you into the key biblical passages on the subject of marriage.
2. To evaluate the basis for your marriage.
3. To cultivate true spiritual intimacy through your study, discussion, and prayer together.
4. To surface and eliminate potential problems.
5. To equip you with biblical principles that will enable you to cope with problems in your marriage.

How to Use This Study Guide

1. This study guide has been written for you. Begin the program at least four months before your wedding. This will allow sufficient time for your roles to develop, your goals to form, and your relationship to ripen. More than this, it will permit time for supplementary reading and, when possible, counseling appointments.

2. As much as is possible do each of the assignments together as a couple.

3. Do not hurry! The object is not to complete the course. It is to build a relationship. Pray together over each assignment. Spend time reading the material together and discussing the content. Interact with one another. Challenge the text. Apply the material to yourself openly and honestly. Assist your partner in his/her efforts to evaluate and apply the lessons.

4. To supplement your reading and work in this study guide you will be asked to read from three other books during the program. It would be a good investment to purchase these books for your own library in your new home.

Jay Adams   *Christian Living in the Home* (Nutley, New Jersey: Presbyterian and Reformed Publishing Company, 1972).

Larry Christenson   *The Christian Family* (Minneapolis: Bethany Fellowship, 1970).

Tim LaHaye   *The Act of Marriage*
                          (Grand Rapids: Zondervan Pub-
                          lishing House, 1976).

5. Although this study guide may be done by the two of you
   alone, it has been designed to be used in conjunction
   with a marriage counselor.

   If possible, approach the minister who will officiate at
   your wedding, or some other competent counselor, and
   ask him/her to work with you through the program. Your
   counselor will be a useful "sounding board" and a helpful resource person. In most cases, four counseling ses-
   sions will be sufficient. For a June wedding, the following schedule would be ideal.

Appointment	Month	Preparation for Appointment
First	February	Part One of the study guide. Be sure to have Part One completed for this first session.
Second	March	Complete Part Two of the study guide.
Third	April	Complete Part Three of the study guide.
Fourth	May	Complete Part Four of the study guide.

6. In preparation for your counseling appointments mark in
   the margin of the text points you wish to raise for discussion. Write down questions you want to raise with your
   counselor.

7. Prior to your fourth and last counseling appointment, or
   two months before your wedding, both of you ought to
   have a complete physical examination by a physician. It
   is important to enter marriage with a thorough knowledge of the state of one's own health as well as the health
   of your partner. On this occasion you ought to have determined precisely what you will do regarding the use of
   contraceptives.

18

Let marriage be held in honor among all *(Heb. 13:4)*.

He who finds a wife finds a good thing, and obtains favor from the LORD   *(Prov. 18:22)*.

Compared with marriage
Being born is a mere episode in our careers.
And dying a trivial incident.
—*Dorothy Dix*

The sanctity of marriage and the family relation
make the corner stone of our American society
and civilization.   —*James Abram Garfield*

The Christian religion, by confining marriage to pairs, and rendering the relation indissoluble, has by these two things done more toward the peace, happiness, settlement, and civilization of the world, than by any other part in this whole scheme of divine wisdom.   —*Edmund Burke*

Lord, when we are wrong, make us willing to change. And when we are right, make us easy to live with.   —*Peter Marshall*

Marriage was instituted by God Himself for the purpose of preventing promiscuous intercourse of the sexes, for promoting domestic felicity, and for securing the maintenance and security of children.   —*Noah Webster, An American Dictionary of the English Language, (1828)*

Part One

The Criteria for Marriage

Mike took the old economics book off his shelf. Somehow, when he poured over its pages in diligent study, he never dreamed he would put it to such good use. The razor blade whittled away at the pages until a neat, two-by-two square was carved in its center. He dropped a shiny red and gold box with its precious contents into the hole, and wrapped the mystery package in colorful birthday paper.

It was but two weeks before Christmas. More important, it was Penny's twenty-second birthday. A special evening had been planned. Mike casually but carefully set his gift on the coffee table in the Graham's living room before he left with Penny to enjoy dinner at "L'Auberge de Petit Prince."

Later that evening, in the candlelight of her living room, an unsuspecting Penny unwrapped the brightly flowered paper and was stunned to discover that Mike had given her an economics book, and an old one at that! Perhaps there was an endearing inscription inside. Lifting the cover she spied the little gold box, and then the ring. What a beautiful surprise!

This was the culmination of a romance that had quietly begun ten months earlier. Although they had known each other for the last six years, they had been little more than distant friends in the same youth group of their church. Mike was now completing his undergraduate studies in philosophy and Penny would shortly be writing her exams prior to becoming a registered nurse. Under the good hand of God, their relationship had ripened into a deep and settled commitment to each other. Yet during those months they had often wondered, "Are we ready for marriage?"

It's possible you may have asked yourselves this question a hundred times. Because you are where you are today (engaged and preparing for marriage), it is probably safe to assume you have finally answered the question in the affirmative.

For some, it may be a rather shaky, uncertain, and hesitant "Yes." After all, how can we be sure?

For others, it may be a strong and confident "Yes." But what is the basis of such certainty?

Let's ask the question one last time. There are several specific criteria you ought to consider.

1   The First Priority

I well remember my first encounter with Chris and Diane. They had asked me to marry them. At the beginning of our first premarriage counseling session, I asked them to describe for me briefly their relationship with Jesus Christ. Diane passed with flying colors; there was no doubt she was a believer in the Lord Jesus. But Chris was another matter.

He was vague, perplexed by it all. What a wonderful opportunity for a Christian marriage counselor. As I recall, the grand old story of Jesus and His love was simply told. To illustrate my points I portrayed three scenes with my hands. First, I described

The Original State

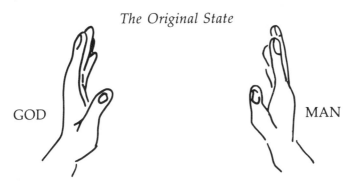

GOD   MAN

In the original state God and man enjoyed a beautiful harmonious relationship and they were in perfect fellowship. Then something came between them. (I used a book to illustrate the point.) Man sinned. Then I presented

The Fallen State

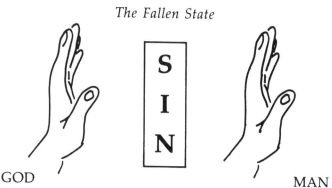

GOD   MAN

Adam turned his back on God when he sinned, and because God is too holy to behold iniquity He turned from man. God and man—back to back. God offended by sin. Man offending by sin. Fellowship was broken. Hostility entered. Communication suffered. Condemnation was certain.

Now, into the drama of human history entered the grace of God.

The Grace State

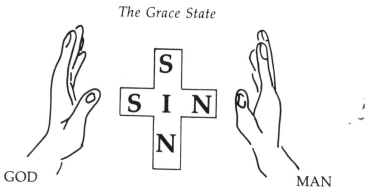

GOD   MAN

Moved by His sovereign purpose and His love for man, God sent to earth His Son, Jesus Christ, to deal forever with the sin that had come between Himself and man. When God, in the person of Jesus Christ, went to the cross at Calvary, He went to deal with the problem of sin. He bore the guilt of man's sin there upon the cross. God the Father punished His Son for the sins of men and women. Because sin has now been judged, because Jesus Christ has paid the debt completely, God's righteousness has been satisfied. His wrath has been appeased. Through the atoning death of Jesus, God has been turned back to man, for He was in Christ reconciling the world to Himself (2 Cor. 5:19).

What remains to be done? In the words of the great apostle Paul:

> Therefore, we are ambassadors for Christ, as though God were entreating through us; we beg you on behalf of Christ, be reconciled to God (2 Cor. 5:20).

We are urged to turn to God and to receive Jesus Christ personally as our Savior. As you turn to God and receive the Lord Jesus, trusting in Him as the One who has died for your sins, your relationship with God is restored. Rather than being an enemy of God, you become a friend and child of God. No longer alienated, you are reconciled to God and become the possessor of His salvation.

That evening I asked Chris if he had ever had the experience of turning to God and receiving Jesus Christ as his personal Savior. He said he did not think so. The decision was left with him. That night he and Diane talked and prayed. Shortly thereafter, he received Jesus Christ as his personal Savior. Chris is now living and serving as an active Christian, but more important than that, he is a partner in a Christian marriage. Both he and his wife are truly born-again believers in our Lord Jesus. This is the first ingredient in a Christian marriage, and three biblical facts make it absolutely essential.

A. THE PICTURE OF MARRIAGE

> Wives, be subject to your own husbands, as to the Lord. For the husband is the head of the wife, as Christ also is the head of the Church, He Himself being the Savior of the body. But as the church is subject to Christ, so also the wives ought to be to their husbands in everything. Husbands, love your wives, just as Christ also loved the church and gave Himself up for her (Eph. 5:22–25).

Marriage represents the relationship between Christ and the church and this could never be represented by a marriage where one is a believer and the other is not.

B. The Goal of Marriage

For this cause a man shall leave his father and his mother, and shall cleave to his wife; and they shall become one flesh (Gen. 2:24).

Here is the goal of marriage—two individuals become one. This can never be achieved as long as one is a believer and the other an unbeliever. They may be one physically, emotionally, and socially, but they will never be one spiritually. The believer's spirit is alive and vital, but the unbeliever's spirit is dead. In order for the two to be one in every respect and to enjoy the reality of a Christian marriage they must both be born-again believers in the Lord Jesus.

C. The Instruction for Marriage

Do not be bound together with unbelievers; for what partnership have righteousness and lawlessness, or what fellowship has light with darkness? (2 Cor. 6:14).

The King James version reads, "Be not unequally yoked together with unbelievers." An unequal yoke is the yoke of a believer with an unbeliever. In the context of 2 Corinthians 6, this ought never to exist in a church relationship. But surely there is a principle here that applies to other relationships—marriage, for example. This is clear from other passages of Scripture.

A wife is bound as long as her husband lives; but if her husband is dead, she is free to be married to whom she wishes, only in the Lord (1 Cor. 7:39).

Then it is clear. The first criteria for a Christian marriage is a new birth into the family of God. Recently a distraught wife on the verge of a divorce cried out, "But I thought he was a Christian when we were married!" I asked, "What made you think so?" Listen carefully to her tragic answer. She said, "He told me so." What naiveté! In defense some will say, "But we are not to judge, are we?" My friend, if ever there was a time to judge a person's profession of faith in Christ it is here. The Lord would never instruct you to marry a believer if He did not expect you to evaluate a profession of faith.

How can you know? Examine the fruit! A genuine believer loves the Lord, loves the people of God, loves the Word of God, and loves the work of God. Take a good look. The evidence of spiritual life is spiritual growth. Do you see this in the person you plan to marry? The fruit of the Spirit of God indwelling the believer is love, joy, peace, patience, kindness, goodness, faithfulness, gentleness, self-control (Gal. 5:22–23). There ought to be some evidence of life.

Beware of empty and false professions. Our Lord warned of such things when he said:

> Not every one who says to me, "Lord, Lord," will enter the kingdom of heaven; but he who does the will of My Father who is in heaven. Many will say to Me on that day, "Lord, Lord, did we not prophesy in Your name, and in Your name cast out demons, and in Your name perform many miracles?" And then I will declare to them, "I never knew you, depart from Me, you who practice lawlessness" (Matt. 7:21–23).

Project Page

To be done by the fiancé (male).

1. Do you have the deep conviction that your fiancée is a genuine believer in Jesus Christ?

2. Give a brief resumé of her conversion experience.

3. What evidence do you have that she is a true believer rather than a mere professing Christian?

To be done by the fiancée (female).

4. Do you have the deep conviction that your fiancé is a genuine believer in Jesus Christ?

5. Give a brief resumé of his conversion experience.

6. What evidence do you have that he is a true believer rather than a mere professing Christian?

2 Parental Approval

What a help parents can be and must be when their children are contemplating marriage. Cathy, a lovely Christian young lady, planned to get married. Her fiancé was a fine young man in every way, but one. Even though his father was a minister, he had no interest whatsoever in spiritual matters. Her parents so opposed the marriage that Cathy agreed to cancel it. Twice after that she has come to her mother, put her arms around her, and thanked her for being a "mean mother." She then promised, "When I marry I am going to be a mean mother like you." What a wise young lady! She followed the counsel of her parents.

Parental opposition to a marriage may well be God's way of keeping a child from a hell on earth. Many times I have heard, "If I had only listened to them!" Parents have gone down the road. They often are more objective because they have had the experience. Generally, the welfare of their child is their greatest concern.

Parental opposition to a marriage may well be God's way of telling a child to wait. He could be saying, "It's not on My schedule for your life at this time. This is not according to My timetable." There is no clearer and better way to say this than through parents. If it is God's will that a couple wait, be assured there is a wise and good reason! How foolish to challenge God's wisdom!

The blessing of parents on a marriage is of immense value —before the marriage, during the marriage, and in the years following the marriage. The happiness of a marriage is both deeper and broader when the parents give their approval.

But is parental approval required? Must there be unqualified support from them? Is this a criterion for marriage? The answer from Scripture seems to be both yes and no.

The responsibility of the Christian child is clear.

> Children, obey your parents in the Lord, for this is right. Honor your father and mother (which is the first commandment with a promise), that it may be well with you, and that you may live long on the earth (Eph. 6:1–3).

The injunction to obey parents is generally understood to apply to children as long as they are living under their parents' roof or are living on their parents' income. In such situations children certainly are obliged to honor their parents by obeying them. Unqualified approval ought to be obtained before marriage is entered.

And yet, it surely is the responsibility of children to give honor as long as their parents live. Even after Christian children leave their parents' domestic and financial shelter they may honor them by seeking their counsel and approval. What if, in such cases, approval is not forthcoming? Can the marriage be pursued? Or should plans be abandoned? The evidence of Scripture seems to indicate that one's spiritual relationship with Christ in the family of God does supersede natural relationships.

> And answering them, He said, "Who are My mother and My brothers?" And looking about on those who were sitting around Him, He said, "Behold, My mother and My brothers! For whoever does the will of God, he is My brother and sister and mother" (Mark 3:33–35).

> If anyone comes to Me, and does not hate his own father and mother and wife and children and brothers and sisters, yes, and even his own life, he cannot be My disciple (Luke 14:26).

Discipleship and dedication to Jesus Christ sometimes involve a commitment to Him above the commitment to our parents. Whenever a child is tempted to move apart from parental approval, he must be very careful that his reason for doing so is his dedication to Christ.

If a person is to enter into a marriage relationship apart from the approval of his parents, it could be because of his higher allegiance to Jesus Christ. He recognizes that it is his faith in Christ which has become a barrier in his relationship to his parents.

There may well be other exceptions. A jealous father, a selfish mother, an apostate parent, and many other "reasons" can become barriers to a Christian wedding. In such circumstances young couples are urged to move cautiously, thoughtfully, considerately, and prayerfully.

Project Page

1. Fiancé—Briefly describe your parents' attitude toward your proposed marriage.

2. Fiancée—Briefly describe the attitude of your parents toward your proposed marriage.

3. In what positive ways have you honored your parents through the process of your engagement?

4. What concrete steps do you plan to take to gain or ensure the support of your parents for your wedding and married life?

3   Tests of Love

Several months ago a young couple with severe marital problems sought help. After the husband had told his tale of woe, he sighed and said, "I guess we just weren't ready to get married."

Many aren't, but realize it too late.

When is a couple ready for marriage?

"When we are sure we are in love!" This is the standard answer today. For most, love is the sole criterion for marriage. Yet many couples can hardly identify it, let alone define it.

To be told, "Oh, you'll know when it hits you; it hits you right between the eyes; you'll know when it is the real thing," leaves you a helpless slave to a master you can't even identify. There are however, some time-proven tests of true, genuine love, the kind of love that builds great marriages.

In his book, *I Married You*, Walter Trobisch has suggested six tests for love.[1]

1. *The Sharing Test.* Are you able to share together? Do you want to make your partner happy or do you want to become happy?
2. *The Strength Test.* Does your love give you new strength and fill you with creative energy? Or does it take away your strength and energy?
3. *The Respect Test.* Do you really have respect for each other? Are you proud of your partner?
4. *The Habit Test.* Do you only love each other or do you also like each other and accept each other with your habits and shortcomings?

5. *The Quarrel Test.* Are you able to forgive each other and give in to each other? The ability to be reconciled after a real quarrel must be tested before marriage.
6. *The Time Test.* "Never get married until you have summered and wintered with your partner." Has your love summered and wintered? Do you know each other long enough to know each other well enough?

To these six tests four others may be added.

7. *The Separation Test.* Do you feel an unusual joy while in the company of each other? Is there pain in separation?
8. *The Giving Test.* Love and marriage are giving, not getting. Are you in love to give? Are you capable of self-giving? Is this quality of self-giving constantly evident?
9. *The Growth Test.* Is your love dynamic in its growth? Is it progressively maturing? Are the characteristics of Christian love developing?
10. *The Sex Test.* Is there a mutual enjoyment of each other without the constant need of physical expression? If you can't be together without petting, you don't have the maturity and love essential for marriage.

Dr. Howard Hendricks, writing on "Yardsticks for Love," expands upon this last test:

It is lamentable to see so many who think that the only thing that embraces true love is to hang all over each other. Studies show that promiscuity before marriage is the best preparation for promiscuity in marriage, and purity before marriage is the best guarantee for purity in marriage. Furthermore, those who can't get together without physical expression before their marriage will often have no physical expression after the first year. Why? Because they have never really built an adequate basis for their relationship—no real companionship, no real commonality, nothing that they can share other than the body.

Walter Trobisch offers this profound insight:

Sex is no test of love for it is precisely the very thing that one wants to test which is destroyed by the testing.[2]

Mutual respect becomes damaged, and emptiness creeps into the relationship. The couple becomes less and less sure of their love. So they intensify their intimacies in the hope of intensifying their love, but in so doing they become less sure of their love.

Consider for a moment Paul's description of the manifestations of true love.

> Love is patient, love is kind, and is not jealous; love does not brag and is not arrogant, does not act unbecomingly; it does not seek its own, is not provoked, does not take into account a wrong suffered, does not rejoice in unrighteousness, but rejoices with the truth; bears all things, believes all things, hopes all things, endures all things (1 Cor. 13:4-7).

Love is the unconditional acceptance of a person, flaws and all. It therefore demands a thorough knowledge of that person, a recognition of strengths and weaknesses, and acceptance.

Put it to the test. Examine it carefully. You are not ready for marriage until it is evident that your relationship is based on a genuine love for each other.

Notes

[1]Walter Trobisch, *I Married You* (New York: Harper and Row, 1971), pp. 75-77.
[2]Ibid., p. 77.

- the KJV renders "is not provoked" as " is not easily provoked"
- also renders "does not take into account a wrong suffered" as "thinketh no evil"

38

Project Page

1. Review the ten tests of genuine love. Check off the ones you pass.

2. List below the tests of love that must be given a less than satisfactory grade in your relationship. Be honest with yourselves!

3. Having scrutinized 1 Corinthians 13:4–7 carefully from every possible angle, can you really say yours is a true Christian love for each other? Below, make a list of the characteristics from this passage that are clearly evident in your relationship—and another list of those that are less evident.

4   Marriage Is for Grown-Ups

Why is it that 75 percent of teen-age marriages end in divorce? Why will any marriage counselor tell you that most marriage problems are a result of immaturity? It is because marriage is for grown-ups.

This may come as a surprise to many of our young people, but consider the evidence.

> For this cause a man shall leave his father and his mother, and shall cleave to his wife; and they shall become one flesh (Gen. 2:24).

It is a man who is to leave his father and mother, for he must assume the responsibility of establishing and heading a new family unit. The precedent for this is set by scores of biblical marriages. Marriage is for adults—persons who have reached a level of maturity adequate for the situation.

What havoc is caused by emotional immaturity. Its hidden rocks have shipwrecked scores of marriages. It is the secret spring from which flows the most destructive forces on earth. Consider these indicators of emotional immaturity.

1. Inability to compromise
2. Cruelty, either physical or mental
3. Self-pity
4. Compulsive revenge-taking
5. Excusing self and self-defense
6. Violent quarreling
7. Lack of a sense of responsibility
8. Misuse of authority
9. Scorn for religious background
10. Dependence on feelings alone[1]

The presence of any two or three of these indicators predicts a stormy marriage ahead. Marriage is a relationship for the mature.

Study briefly four signs of emotionally mature persons.

1. *They Are Realistic.* They see themselves, life, and others as they really are. There is an absence of fantasy, dreams, and escape flights. They have an accurate appraisal of their assets and liabilities.
2. *They Are Able to Adjust to Circumstances.* There is a flexibility and ability to adjust to pressure or ease, poverty or plenty, responsibility or freedom, and a thousand other circumstnaces that may haunt the tracks of a married couple.
3. *They Are Able to Control Their Emotions.* Self-control is a mark of maturity. The entire spectrum of the emotions is involved. Emotionally mature persons have control over love, hate, jealousy, temper, pride, depression, moods, etc. It is not difficult to imagine the worth of such a quality in any home.
4. *They Are Able to Give Themselves in Intimate Friendships or Love.*

Failure in any of these four areas spells problems for a marriage. But physical and emotional maturity are not sufficient; for a Christian marriage to be successful spiritual maturity must also be considered.

> For every one who partakes only of milk is not accustomed to the word of righteousness, for he is a babe. But solid food is for the mature, who because of practice have their senses trained to discern good and evil (Heb. 5:13–14).

Three marks of spiritual maturity are discernable from our text.

1. Spiritual maturity belongs to those who have their senses trained to discern good and evil. What a wonderful asset this is to any marriage.
2. Spiritual maturity is the result of careful and long practice. This doesn't happen overnight. The new convert is a babe in Christ and needs time to grow before entering into marriage.

3. *Spiritual maturity involves a capacity for solid food, that is, Bible doctrines in some depth.*

Obviously then, a spiritually mature person is one who knows the Word of God, is able to use the Word of God independently, and on the basis of his knowledge and use of the Word is able to discern between good and evil, or between better and best. He is a person of spiritual discernment.

Being ready for marriage involves having an adequate level of physical, emotional, and spiritual maturity.

Are you ready?

Notes

[1]Frank Peters, "Marriage Is for Grown-Ups," *Eternity Magazine* (August, 1973), pp. 21–23.

Project Page

1. What indications of immaturity are evident in your personal lives as individuals?

2. Trace the problems you have in your present relationship to their source. What aspects of immaturity are the root of these problems?

3. Understanding that the process of maturing involves more than just time, what steps are you taking toward maturing emotionally and spiritually?

The Criteria for Marriage

"Are we ready for marriage?"

To ask that question intelligently is to be concerned with four areas: the nature of your relationship to Jesus Christ, the approval of your parents, the genuineness of your love, and the level of your maturity. These are solid and solemn criteria for entering into a Christian marriage.

Now summarize your conclusions.

THE CRITERIA	YOUR CONCLUSION
NEW BIRTH	
PARENTAL APPROVAL	
GENUINE LOVE	
MATURITY	

Projects for Next Month

1. Complete Part Two of your study guide.
2. Read: Jay Adams, *Christian Living in the Home*, pp. 47–56.

   Larry Christenson, *The Christian Family*, chs. 1, 2, 5.

3. If you are working with a marriage counselor, be prepared to go through the Scriptures explaining your respective responsibilities as a Christian wife/husband. Be ready to discuss to what degree these roles are emerging in your relationship.

Part Two

Christian Marriage

SEVEN BASICS

Compared with marriage, being born is a mere episode of our career and dying a trivial incident.

These perceptive words come from the pen of Dorothy Dix, America's foremost female counselor of a few years ago. She is saying that there is no more crucial, important, or critical step in our social life than the step into marriage—and this is hard to debate.

Marriage is that one giant step that takes us into a life either of deep fulfillment or desperate frustration. The outcome is largely determined by our concept of marriage.

To cultivate a correct concept, or perhaps, to correct a corrupted concept, let us dissect carefully and digest the key Old Testament passage on marriage.

Then the LORD God said, "It is not good for the man to be alone; I will make him a helper suitable for him." And out of the ground the LORD God formed every beast of the field and every bird of the sky, and brought them to the man to see what he would call them; and whatever the man called a living creature that was its name. And the man gave names to all the cattle, and to the birds of the sky, and to every beast of the field, but for Adam there was not found a helper suitable for him. So the LORD God caused a deep sleep to fall upon the man, and he slept; then He took one of his ribs, and closed up the flesh at that place. And the LORD God fashioned into a woman the rib which He had taken from the man, and brought her to the man. And the man said, "This is bone of my bones, and flesh of my flesh; she shall be called Woman, because she was taken out of Man." For this cause a man shall leave his father and his mother, and shall cleave to his wife; and they shall become one flesh (Gen. 2:18–24).

Woven into the lines of these verses are seven facts basic to a concept of a Christian marriage. These principles provide the framework for the next seven chapters.

5   In the Beginning

Marriage is an institution established by God. This is the first implication of the Genesis text.

It is quite wrong to imagine that somewhere in a cave around a flickering fire one night a group of previously promiscuous people decided that marriage might be a good idea. It is not a social contract that people worked out and found useful to society for a while.[1]

Society did not invent marriage. We received it from God.

It was God who made Adam. It was God who said, "It is not good for the man to be alone." It was God who made Eve. It was God who brought her to Adam.

Adam did not take a wife—he received a wife. God gave away the first bride and officiated at the first wedding ceremony. Thus, marriage is a divine institution. This being the case, two conclusions are unavoidable.

FIRST, WE CANNOT DISCARD IT

Recently someone said, "Now that we have the pill and have legalized abortion, most of the usefulness of marriage has disappeared." A national magazine reported a poll at Mills College which indicated 40 percent of the female seniors did not consider marriage important.[2] In Sweden today marriage is going out of style.

But a divine institution cannot be discarded so easily. No legislature, no society, no individual has the right to set aside what God has set up—to eliminate what God has established. Only God who instituted it can abrogate it, and this He has not done.

While some today have discarded marriage as one would discard an outgrown garment, others are radically redefining it. But if it is a divine institution how shall we define it?

SECOND, WE MUST DEFINE IT IN GOD'S TERMS

Another national periodical declares, "From coast to coast married swingers are experimenting with a radical redefinition of marriage."[3] It reports that more than two million middle-class Americans participate in some form of group sex.

In her book, *The Single Parent Experience*, Carol Klein observes that the family is in trouble, and people are experimenting with and redefining the family. She speaks of single women in their late twenties, not married, who have decided to have a baby. Rather than coercing the man they were with or marrying someone they did not love, they became mothers independently.[4] Single women adopting children, or purposely becoming pregnant without any plans for marriage, are remarkable phenomena of our age.

We dare not define marriage from a perverted production of Hollywood, nor from a popular paperback in the drugstore, nor by a promiscuous person in the office or on campus. God, who has instituted it, has also defined it. Marriage, God's style, is monogamous: one husband and one wife. The husband is to cleave to his wife, not wives (Gen. 2:24). The two, not three or four, are to become one (Matt. 19:5).

Marriage, after the divine design, is permanent. The husband is to cleave to his wife, be glued to her, stuck to her—not with her! (Gen. 2:24). Our Lord's commentary on this phrase is: "What therefore God has joined together, let no man separate" (Matt. 19:6).

Biblical marriage is an exclusive relationship, for the two are to become one flesh (Gen. 2:24). Forsaking all others, the husband is to be faithful to his wife so long as she lives.

Finally, marriage is a heterosexual relationship. It seems almost incredible that such a point need be made. Yet, it does need to be made—more today than ever before. Marriage consists of one husband and one wife.

It is into this kind of union that children are to be born. The injunction to be fruitful and multiply was addressed to a married couple. It is within the framework of a home with two parents that children are to be reared.

Marriage is an institution of God. We cannot discard it. We dare not redefine it. We accept it as He has established it.

Notes

[1]Jay Adams, *Christian Living In The Home* (Nutley, New Jersey: Presbyterian and Reformed Publishing Co., 1972), p. 44.

[2]*U.S. News and World Report* (June 19, 1972), p. 30.

[3]*Newsweek*, "Group Sex" Vol. 77 (June 21, 1972), pp. 98–99.

[4]See Carol Klein, *The Single Parent Experience* (New York: Walker and Company, 1973).

Project Page

1. How does God define marriage? List the four features that have been isolated in this chapter.

   1.

   2.

   3.

   4.

2. Working together, write your own definition of marriage. Be sure that it reflects the features of Genesis 2:24.

53

6 Completely Perfect

Marriage is a blessing of God. Here is the second observation to be made from the Mosaic account in Genesis 2.

It was the Lord God who said, "It is not good for the man to be alone" (Gen. 2:18). This is the first "not good" in all of God's creative works. Following the provision of Eve for Adam, when the work of creation was completed, "God saw all that He had made, and behold, it was very good" (Gen. 1:31). Von Rad translates, "it was completely perfect."[1] What a difference the creation of Eve made. The provision of a wife for Adam changed a "not good" into a "completely perfect." Marriage is surely one of the most serene and sublime blessings God has bestowed on humanity.

If, indeed, marriage is a blessing of God, three inescapable implications follow:

First, We Ought to Speak Of It Respectfully

Such words are scarce indeed. Wit and senselessness have combined to coin cute but cutting comments about marriage. Do these sound familiar?

> Marriage is a wonderful institution, if you want to spend the rest of your life in an institution.

> If you want a good year marry, if you want two refrain. (A German proverb)

Donald Grey Barnhouse used to say: "Bite your tongue before you will ever say, 'Well, I want you to meet the old ball and chain,' or, in referring to your wife, 'Here comes the jailor.' "

The jokes that ridicule marriage are legion. Many are said innocently, but they are actually not so innocent.

You may adversely affect your children. You may influence them into thinking that marriage, which can be the happiest and most blessed state in life, is all a big mistake.

With your crude comments you may condemn yourself. It is out of the abundance of your heart that your mouth speaks. Many a word said in jest has more than a kernel of truth in it!

You may corrupt and disrupt your marriage with your innocent statements of ridicule. Such words frequently cut deeply, and they leave wounds that do not heal, doubts that linger, resentments that fester.

Beware because you may be conditioning, even now, the one you love. In the course of time some marriage partners eventually come to see themselves as they have been portrayed. Your marriage will suffer and you will be the loser.

Most serious of all, however, is that such talk contradicts God. What He says is "very good," you are saying is not good after all. Dr. Walter Maier writes:

> To speak disdainfully of married life, to invoke upon it sophisticated sarcasm, is to exalt the puny errors of pigmy minds over the eternal truth of heaven—to blaspheme God.

Begin now to speak of marriage respectfully. Refer to your marriage and your prospective partner in terms that will reflect your understanding that marriage is one of your richest blessings from God. This is the first implication.

SECOND, WE OUGHT TO ESTEEM IT HIGHLY

In the light of Paul's teaching in 1 Corinthians 7 some have concluded that celibacy is commended as a higher state than marriage. After all, Paul says, "He who gives his own virgin daughter in marriage does well, and he who does not give her in marriage will do better" (1 Cor. 7:38).

Of course he does. But this is not to be understood as a generalization. This is in view of the particular situation in Corinth. According to verse 26, a blood bath seemed imminent. Because of the expected persecution, the apostle proposed that it would be better to remain single.

Christian Marriage

Charles Hodge says Paul wrote to Corinth as one would speak to an army about to enter into an unequal conflict in the enemy's country for a prolonged period of time—this is not the time to marry![2]

Celibacy is not commended as a higher state here or anywhere in Scripture. Marriage is good, a great blessing of God for mankind. As such, it ought to be esteemed highly.

FINALLY, WE OUGHT TO REGARD IT AS HONORABLE

Before the Fall, God said, "Be fruitful and multiply" (Gen. 1:28). After the institution of marriage, He said it was "very good." Many centuries later, to a society plagued by perversion, He said, "Let marriage be held in honor among all" (Heb. 13:4).

The marriage bed is undefiled. Sex within marriage is good and holy. Paul parallels the marriage relationship to the holy union existing between Christ and His church. Our Lord spoke of His relationship to His people as that of a bridegroom to a bride (Rev. 12:7–9; 21:2).

Nothing could be clearer. God considers marriage to be holy, righteous, and good. So ought we. It is a blessing of God.

Notes

[1]Gerhard von Rad, *Genesis* (London: S.C.M. Press Ltd., 1972), p. 61.
[2]Charles Hodge, *Commentary on the First Epistle to the Corinthians* (Grand Rapids: Eerdmans, 1969), p. 112.

Project Page

1. Circle the phrase that best describes the *attitude* toward marriage you generally communicate.

> needs no improvement
> highly respectful
> moderately respectful
> inconsistent
> irreverent
> disrespectful
> highly inadequate

2. What three things will you both decide to do now to communicate a higher regard for this divine blessing and for each other as partners in this institution?

   1.

   2.

   3.

7   Normal or Abnormal?

Marriage is a norm of society. This seems eminently evident from the words of God: "It is not good for the man to be alone" (Gen. 2:18). Subsequent Scripture substantiates this principle. Paul writes "Let each man have his own wife, and let each woman have her own husband" (1 Cor. 7:2). Marriage is a norm of society.

Do singles, then, miss God's best? Hardly. Not when a life of singleness is God's perfect will. And, in some cases, this is obviously so. According to 1 Corinthians 7:7 some have the "gift" of self-control that equips them for a life of singleness. To be "contentedly single" is a live option and a valid alternative for a Spirit-led child of God. In no sense, whatever, is such a role abnormal. And yet, marriage is a norm of society. God's general pattern for living is the family—husband, wife, children. But His general pattern for humanity is not necessarily His pattern for everyone.

I urge young people to plan on marriage unless they are clearly shown otherwise by God. Marriage is a norm, not an exception. Generally it is safe for young people to assume it is God's purpose for them, and accordingly, to make it part of their plans.

Obviously you both have done just this. You are planning on marriage because it is a norm. You would not expect some supernatural or startling sign to point you in this direction. But you ought to expect some confirmation from God that you are going in the right direction with the right person at the right time. Do you have that?

Project Page

In what specific ways has the Lord recently confirmed to you that your marriage at this time is, indeed, His plan for you both?

8 Two's a Company

Marriage is a partnership of two. This is the fourth fact that lies rooted in the text of Genesis 2.

Peter Marshall expressed it this way: "The marriage relationship is the most delightful and the most sacred and solemn of human relations. It is the blending of lives and the union of hearts that two may walk together up the hill of life to meet the dawn together bearing life's burdens and sharing its joys and sorrows."

Four facets of this marital partnership can be ferreted out of the Mosaic mandate for marriage.

FIRST, THE PLANNER OF THE PARTNERSHIP IS GOD

What confidence and reassurance this breeds as you approach your marriage. God is sovereignly in control. He works "*all things* after the counsel of His will" (Eph. 1:11)—even marriages. Do you desire His will, His perfect will in regard to your marriage? This is promised to those who unconditionally and totally commit themselves to His lordship in their lives. Such Christians will prove in their own experience His perfect will, which is good for them and pleasing to God. Listen again to the beseeching plea of the apostle:

> I urge you therefore, brethren, by the mercies of God, to present your bodies a living and holy sacrifice, acceptable to God, which is your spiritual service of worship. And do not be conformed to this world, but be transformed by the renewing of your mind, that you may prove what the will of God is, that which is good and acceptable and perfect (Rom. 12:1-2).

As a young lady, Betty Stam wrote, "Lord, I give up my own purposes and plans, all my own desires, hopes and ambitions (whether they be fleshly or soulish) and accept Thy will for my life. I give myself, my life, my all, utterly to Thee, to be Thine forever. I hand over to Thy keeping all of my friendships. All the people whom I love are to take second place in my heart. Fill me now and seal me with Thy Spirit. Work out Thy whole will in my life, at any cost, now and forever. To me to live is Christ. Amen."

That is dedication.

Few steps in all your lives will be more significant than this one. You say you earnestly yearn for God's perfect will in your lives. Then why not, together, just now, do what the Spirit of God urges you to do in Romans 12:1–2. For this select company there is the reassuring confidence of experiencing His perfect will.

SECOND, THE PURPOSE OF THE PARTNERSHIP IS COMPANIONSHIP

This is surely not the sole purpose of marriage. Marriage was instituted for the propagation of the human race, as well as for the effective administration of the earth. Primarily, however, our text implies it was for companionship.

"It is not good for the man to be alone" (Gen. 2:18).

"She is your companion and your wife by covenant" (Mal. 2:14).

Above all else, marriage is a companionship. I always thrill at the sight of an older couple who are still walking the bridle path hand in hand as good friends. Remember, my friend, a contract may make her your wife, but it will never make her your companion. And yet, this is the purpose of marriage.

The question, then, is not, "Will he be a good provider?" nor, "Does he offer me security?" nor even, "Will she be a good mother for our children?" The question before all of these is this: "Will he be a companion to me?" or, "Am I prepared to be his companion for life?"

Companionship: the primary purpose of marriage. How gracious of God to provide for such a need. How wise to make such a provision.

THIRD, THE PARTNERS OF THE PARTNERSHIP ARE COMPLEMENTARY

"I will make him a helper suitable for him" (Gen. 2:18).

When the Lord said "I will make him a helper," He indicated a basic need of man. To achieve his objectives in life man needs a helper. To fulfill God's design for him, he needs the help of a mate in every way. Alone, man is not only lonely, but he is unable to achieve the two functions given to him by God: subdue the earth, be fruitful and replenish the earth.

When the Lord promised a suitable helper He indicated something about the nature of the helper. Adam's search for an adequate helper from among all the creatures of God proved fruitless. Eve was a distinct work of creation, a special provision, perfectly suited in every way to Adam.

A careful look at this original design for marriage will uncover three things equally true of every marriage that follows the biblical pattern.

1. In her creation she corresponded to him.

This is the implication of the original text. As an image in a mirror corresponds to the object reflected, so the woman corresponds to the man.

Adam recognized her as perfectly corresponding to him, so he acknowledged it with his clever play on words.

> This is now bone of my bones, and flesh of my flesh; she shall be called Woman, because she was taken out of Man (Gen. 2:23).

In the original text "women" is *Isshah* and "man" is *Ish*. The similarity in sound suggests the congruity of Adam and Eve. She alone corresponded to him, and she did it on five levels: physically, emotionally, socially, intellectually, and spiritually.

2. In her marriage she completed him.

Dr. Haddon Robinson well says, "Marriage is more than an outward unity of a man and woman, it is more than two people sharing the same name and living in the same house. The two personalities are joined so that they become the male and female parts of a single entity."

This is the goal of marriage—"one flesh"—oneness!

A phenomenon of our present age is the unprecedented number of Jews who are turning to Christ. Popularly they are known as part of the "Jews for Jesus" movement. They prefer to be called "Messianic Jews" or "Completed Jews." A completed Jew—what a beautiful term. Without Christ—incomplete; with Christ—complete. So also Adam. Apart from Eve he was incomplete. In their marriage he was completed.

Many attempts have been made to illustrate this point. One of the best is the picture presented by an orange cut into two parts by means of a rough irregular slice. Here are two parts that precisely correspond to one another, and, when brought together, perfectly complete each other.

physically
emotionally
socially
intellectually
spiritually

3. After their marriage she complemented him.

This is clearly implied in our text and is surely the divine intent of the marriage. The physical weaknesses of Eve were balanced by the strengths of Adam. The emotional deficiencies of one were balanced by the assets of the other. The social inclinations of both were designed to achieve a balance.

The infinite wisdom of God is supremely seen, not in the creation of a full-bloom rose, nor a precision-timed universe, nor even a human body, but in the creation of a man and a woman to complete each other with a perfect balance.

Marriage is not a partnership of two identical people. What could be more self-destructive than the union of two perfectionists or two totally impatient persons! Some similarities in personalities repel each other as common poles of two magnets. True incompatibility is not two unlike persons being able to tolerate each other's strengths and weaknesses, but rather two similar people unable to adjust to a personality identical to theirs.

God, in His divine and infinite wisdom, makes a wife to

correspond to a husband, brings her to him to complete him, uses her to complement him.

> Oh, the depth of the riches both of the wisdom and knowledge of God! How unsearchable are His judgments and unfathomable His ways! (Rom. 11:33).

One last aspect of the marriage partnership remains to be considered.

FOURTH, THE PROVISION IMPLIES CARE

> He took one of his ribs . . . (Gen. 2:21).

> God fashioned into a woman the rib which He had taken from the man . . . (Gen. 2:22).

From the beginning of biblical history testimony abounds to the dignity and equality of a woman. She was made of no inferior substance but of the same substance as the man.

The Jewish rabbis used to say that Eve was made not from Adam's boot to be trampled down, nor from his head to rule her, but from his rib, near his heart, to be loved, and under his arm to be protected.

The better basis for Adam's love and care for Eve, however, was the fact that she was made from him. She was actually part of him. John Calvin, the great reformer, wrote:

> . . . something was taken from Adam in order that he might embrace, with greater benevolence a part of himself. He lost, therefore, one of his ribs, but instead of it, a far richer reward was granted him, since he obtained a faithful associate in life; for he now saw himself who had before been imperfect rendered complete by his wife."[1]

What is implied in Genesis 2 is an imperative in Ephesians 5. Paul urges every husband to love his wife and nourish and cherish her as he does his own self. Why? Because she is part of him. What a mystery! What a marvel! The wife becomes part of the husband. One entity with a male and female part.

Notes

[1]John Calvin, *Calvin's Commentaries* (Grand Rapids: Associated Publishers and Authors, Inc.), I, 26.

Project Page

1. Are you able to isolate the obstacles in the way to true and genuine companionship? Each of you list the two most prominent ones.

Fiancé

1.

2.

Fiancée

1.

2.

2. What are you prepared to do about these now? List four specific things you will introduce into your relationship for the express purpose of cultivating companionship.

1.

2.

3.

4.

3. In what five specific ways has God's wisdom been demonstrated in bringing you together and giving you to each other for marriage? How do you complement each other?

   1.

   2.

   3.

4.

5.

4. Each of you list three specific things your partner can do to help you now.

Fiancé   *Fiancée*

1.   1.

2.   2.

3.   3.

5. List several specific ways you, even now, can begin to show you care for your fiancée.

    1.

    2.

    3.

    4.

    5.

6. Genesis 2:18–24 contains the divine design for marriage. Restate the four features on which we have thus far focused.

   Marriage is 1.

        2.

        3.

        4.

7. What questions have been raised in your mind through this study that you would like to ask and discuss?

9   The Timeless Triangle

Now for the most important verse in all the Bible on marriage.

It is the most quoted text in all of Scripture on the subject. Four times it is repeated in the New Testament (Matt. 19:5; Mark 10:7; 1 Cor. 6:16; Eph. 5:31).

On the doctrine of marriage no verse is more neglected and misunderstood than this one.

> For this cause a man shall leave his father and his mother, and shall cleave to his wife; and they shall become one flesh (Gen. 2:24).

Obviously, it is a directive with three parts. Walter Trobisch helpfully uses the figure of a triangle to portray the truth of this text.[1]

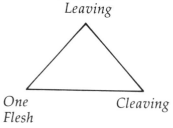

Leaving

One Flesh   *Cleaving*

Here are three essentials for every marriage. They constitute the last three principles to be derived from our Genesis 2 text. Your marriage will be only as strong as the weakest of these three points.

It will come as no surprise to say that marriage involves a "leaving." What "leaving" involves, however, may be more than a little jolting.

Your marriage will never be what God intends it to be without a "leaving." An analysis of this step will produce six significant elements.

First, It Means a Separation

A geographic separation is the most obvious aspect of this "leaving." You are to leave the home of your father and mother and establish a new home, a new family unit. This is affirmed both by precept and practice throughout the Word of God. It is at the peril of the partnership that such a directive is ignored or violated. But this, surely, does not cover the scope of the separation that is in view in this directive.

More than geographic, there is also to be an economic separation. Financial independence of parents is a most desirable ingredient. Occasionally this is practically impossible in the early years of a marriage. Such situations ought always to be considered as temporary and as exceptions. You cannot be the established head of your home as long as you are economically dependent on your parents. Your wife will not respect you as her head when she is constantly looking to her parents for finances. But even this does not plumb the depths of your separation.

Most important of all is the psychological separation. You must leave your parents. Your relationship with them must change. It can no longer continue as it was: parent-child. It must be severed effectively. Many of your earlier ties must be broken. The husband who is constantly comparing his wife with his mother has not left his mother yet. The wife whose parents are still her confidants has not yet left her mother and father.

Leaving, of course, does not mean abandoning. Christian children are responsible to honor their parents as long as they live. But at marriage, they must leave. There can be no real marriage without it.

Second, It Includes Both Partners

At first glance one may think otherwise from our text. Admittedly, it says, "a man shall leave. . . ." For the newly married husband, this is both a word of emancipation and of instruction. Here is a law of life for all humanity granting to sons a free departure from their ancestral home. In this word, parents are instructed to let their son leave, while sons are instructed to depart. This becomes particularly

71

meaningful against a cultural setting in which the wife left her home to take up residence with her new husband in quarters that were often a part of his parents' home. In such a situation the danger of never breaking away from his parents was ever present.

While the husband's attachment to his wife, and her priority in his life, are established in Genesis 2:24, the wife's attachment to her husband and his priority in her life is established in Genesis 3:16. Both are to leave their parents.

What a delight it is to see this expressed meaningfully in a wedding ceremony. The giving away of the bride by both her parents takes on a new significance. As the bride kisses her father and mother she is not only expressing a deep love and eternal gratitude but also a sincere intention—the intention to leave her parents on all three levels. Why should not the groom also signify his love and intention to his parents? A warm handshake and a tender hug will say this loudly and clearly in any ceremony.[2]

THIRD, IT PROVIDES A CONTEXT FOR GROWING

Just as a newborn baby cannot grow up unless the umbilical cord is cut, just so a marriage cannot grow up and develop so long as no real leaving, no clear separation from one's family takes place.[3]

Of primary importance, it provides the context for growing together. After both have left, the new partnership can really grow. The decision has been made—your wife does come before your parents, or, your husband is now your head. The question of a divided allegiance is settled. You have left your parents and committed yourselves to each other. Although outside influences may attempt to intrude, neither of you will permit such a thing. You have left your mothers and fathers and so have eliminated the largest proportion of the proverbial in-law problem. Without leaving, an obstacle to true oneness is carried into your marriage. With leaving, the obstacle is removed. What is left but to grow together?

Of secondary importance, it provides a context for growing independent of parents. Such independence eliminates a major hurdle. The mother-in-law problem is among the major causes for marriage disasters. Contrary to popular opinion the usual conflict is between the wife and her mother-in-law. Far too often his mother cannot be convinced that a young wife is able to care for her precious son and grandchildren. It is only the couple who has genuinely left that will ever become independent of their parents. Such independence is absolutely indispensable.

It is only as you take this route that you will grow together into a deep love relationship and grow up to help your parents in later life.

It is no easy thing to leave—

FOURTH, IT INVOLVES HARDSHIP FOR BOTH PARENTS AND CHILDREN

It has often been observed that all tears shed at weddings are not tears of joy. Some are tears of sorrow, and rightly so. It is painful for many parents to let go. It is no easier for many children to leave. Often it is "with joy and sorrow mingling."

Friends often try to kill the pain by reminding parents they have not lost a son, but gained a daughter. While there is a measure of truth here there is so much error that it becomes a hazard to all concerned to say such a thing. The truth must be faced. Irrespective of the hardship, there must be a leaving and letting go. This is the price of marital prosperity.

FIFTH, IT IS INDICATED BY A PUBLIC ACT

It has well been said that "Marriage is never a private affair." In the ancient Bible world the "leaving" of the bride was a public ceremony. The "leaving" of the groom was a great festive occasion. It is always a public act—parents letting go, children leaving. You will surely want to keep this function of your ceremony uppermost in your mind as you make your plans and come to the altar. To your friends and neighbors you are publicly indicating your leaving of your parents for one another.

FINALLY, IT IMPLIES THE PARENT-CHILD RELATIONSHIP IS TEMPORARY

Our text talks of breaking up something that is temporary—leaving—in favor of joining together something that is permanent—cleaving.

In a practical sense God intends the parent-child relationship to be temporary. Technically, a child never ceases to be a child. His responsibility to honor his parents is a life-long obligation and yet, at marriage, God intends a change to come into that relationship. His former obedience to his parents is no longer there. No longer is she under the headship of her father. No longer are they to care for her, bringing her up in this instruction and discipline of the Lord. That relationship is temporary.

This text is absolute dynamite! Do not pass on too quickly to the second point of this timeless triangle. Pause for a few minutes to reflect on the issues. The project page will help you.

Notes

[1]Walter Trobisch, *I Married You* (New York: Harper and Row, 1971), p. 19.

[2]For a practical suggestion regarding your wedding ceremony see Appendix E.

[3]Walter Trobisch, *I Married You*, p. 13.

Project Page

1. Fiancé: Circle which aspect of leaving will be most difficult for you.

   geographically   economically   psychologically

   Fiancée: Underline which will be most difficult for you.

   Together set out three specific steps you will begin to take now in preparation for an effective "leaving" at your wedding.

   1.

   2.

   3.

2. What can you both plan to do in your ceremony that will communicate your intention to leave your parents?

Christian Marriage

3. Which phrase best describes your parents' attitude toward letting you go? (fiancé—circle, fiancée—underline)

very healthy   tolerant   moderately willing
very resistant   possessive

4. What definite procedures can be implemented now to help cultivate a more healthy attitude on the part of your parents?

10 Stuck, for Life!

Although most Christian husbands would never consider themselves stuck with their wives, yet, biblically, they are stuck to them. This is the implication of "cleaving" in our text.

For this cause a man shall leave his father and his mother, and shall cleave to his wife; and they shall become one flesh (Gen. 2:24).

Leaving	Cleaving
The old relationship Parent-Child Temporary	The new relationship Husband-Wife Permanent

Literally, the verb used by Moses means "to cling to," "to stick to," or "to be glued to." Clearly implied here are three truths that have been largely lost in our secular society.

First, It Indicates That Marriage Is a Monogamous Relationship

Recently in California, Michael, Janice, and Karen were married! A trio marriage! This is not an isolated case, nor is it a biblical concept of marriage.

You are to cleave to your wife—not wives. Genesis 2:24 is a divine directive, and a direct attack against the polygamy of Abraham and Jacob. But it was openly violated by the polygamy of David and Solomon. God never commanded or commended such procedures. A careful study of each case reveals the tragic consequences that often resulted from such unions.

Our Lord's interpretation of this phrase is surely significant. In all four quotations of Genesis 2:24 found in the New Testament the text concludes, "the two shall become one flesh." Marriage is a union of two, and only two.

SECOND, IT INDICATES THAT MARRIAGE IS AN EXCLUSIVE RELATIONSHIP

Several years ago *Newsweek* magazine reported that there were more than two million middle-class American's who were engaged in some form of group sex. "From coast to coast married swingers are experimenting with a radical redefinition of marriage."[1] Marriage alternatives today include open marriage, swinging, cohabitation, cooperative living, group marriages, and intimate networks. These are not Christian concepts of marriage. If you take God seriously then you will take His commandment seriously: "You shall not commit adultery" (Exod. 20:14). You will also take His warning seriously: "Fornicators and adulterers God will judge" (Heb. 13:4). You will ". . . abstain from sexual immorality" (1 Thess. 4:3). Fidelity within marriage, as well as chastity before marriage, is a biblical Christian concept of marriage.

I wonder why God in His Word has some thirty-eight times forbidden premarital or extramarital sex? Every evidence to every sane person is that it is to protect things that are valuable. He wants to protect our *physical* health. It is staggering that with all of our advanced medicine venereal disease in the United States is increasing at a runaway rate.[2]

He also wants to protect our *mental* health. Max Levin, psychiatrist and neurologist in New York City, writes:

> I am among those who regard premarital chastity as the desirable ideal to hold up to our youngsters. As a physician I speak solely from the standpoint of health. Premarital intercourse is hazardous, not so much because of the risk of venereal disease and pregnancy, but because of its threat to emotional health. It is not necessary to spell out the details to the coed who slept with her boy friend in the hope that it would bind them together and lead them to the altar and woke up disillusioned a few months later when he threw her aside for another girl. Her dreams of a rosy future were shattered, and she suffered an emotional trauma from which she might never recover.[3]

More than this, He wants to protect our *marriage*. Premarital sex always brings a barrier into marriage. Extramarital sex fractures a relationship that has been established in marriage.

But most of all, He wants to protect our *relationship with God*. Sexual immorality always leads to such a guilt in one's heart that the first thing that goes is a person's communion with God.

We must also see that He wants to protect our *society*. It can be demonstrated from history that "no society has ever survived after its family life deteriorated."[4]

These are the reasons why God has established for marriage and premarriage the principles of fidelity and chastity. This suggests, as a good friend of mine often says, that there is a sense in which we never break God's laws. Rather, we break ourselves against His laws. There is a sound biblical basis for the vow to "Keep thee only unto her so long as ye both shall live." This is a Christian concept of marriage.

THIRD, IT INDICATES THAT MARRIAGE IS A PERMANENT RELATIONSHIP

Every day in the United States of America more than two thousand marriages are dissolved either by divorce or by separation. In the opinion of many, one of the most serious things that is happening in the United States is that young people are entering into marriage with the idea that it can be terminated. There is every indication that by the time my children reach marriageable age five-year renewable marriage licenses will be available in this country. Again, this is not a Christian concept of marriage. Our Lord's commentary on the institution of marriage is this: "What therefore God has joined together, let no man separate" (Matt. 19:6). Malachi 2:16 clearly states that God hates divorce. It is true that God permits divorce on some very rare occasions, but He never commands it. He never approves. It always violates the divine ideal. Divorce is not part of God's program for marriage. It is generally an unbiblical response to a problem and therefore only creates more problems.

As Christian young people approach marriage one of the most important things they must carefully determine is whether their prospective partners have a biblical concept of marriage. Such a view of marriage must involve these three elements: monogamy, absolute fidelity, and permanency. Marriage is a relationship between two people—only two people—for life.

"When you leave—cleave!"

Marriage is for life—nothing less.

When you marry, you are stuck—for life! But relax. Under the good hand of God it will be your greatest blessing on earth.

Recently I came across an article that captured the truth of Genesis 2:24 in a helpful way.[5] It was called

God's Original Rule for Matrimony:

LEAVE your parents

PHYSICALLY

When you marry, move! (Gen. 2:24) Marriage is the creation under God of a new entity, a new unit of society's oldest and foremost institution. Parent/child relationships are temporary; husband/wife relationship is enduring.

EMOTIONALLY

John 2:4—Parents often want to manipulate their mature children, but adulthood, and especially matrimony, places individuals outside the control of parents to act as responsible parties. Cut the apron strings!

FINANCIALLY

A man's heart should be welded to his wife: so that's where his treasure should be. Too bad when there's financial dependence on parents which

CLEAVE to your wife

LEGALLY

Common law marriages are sin! Biblically, marriage is seen as a contract of covenant under God (Prov. 2:17; Mal. 2:14). Any conjugal relationship apart from lawful marriage is subject to the judgment of God.

INTELLIGENTLY

Scripture gives marriage meaning transcending mere physical or social values. Ephesians 5:32 is the secret: every matrimony portrays the union of Christ and the church. So there's willing submission by the wife and much love from the husband.

PERMANENTLY

"What therefore God hath joined together, let not man put asunder" (Matt. 19:6). The bonds of matrimony ought not divides the heart. Young marrieds should remember if a man does not work, neither should he eat (2 Thess. 3:10). to be broken. This is a permanent relationship, divinely instituted, to be maintained until the death of one of the partners or the Lord returns (Rom. 7:2).

Notes

[1]*Newsweek,* "Group Sex," Vol. 77 (June 21, 1971), pp. 98–99.
[2]*Time,* "Public Health" (Sept. 1, 1967), p. 32.
[3]Max Levin, M.D. "Sex Education," *Current Medical Digest* (May, 1969), pp. 401–402.
[4]*Time,* (Dec. 28, 1970), p. 34.
[5]*Listening,* Vol. 6, No. 5 (London, Canada: Master's House, May, 1977).

Project Page

1. Think carefully. What specific problems will surely appear if parents consider their children a higher priority than their spouse? Remember the implications of leaving—cleaving.

   To the child before marriage.

   To the husband-wife relationship before the marriage of their child.

   To the child at marriage.

   To the parents at the marriage of their child.

   To the child after marriage.

To the parents after the marriage of their child.

2. Think creatively. In what specific ways will you demonstrate to your children, employer, parents, and friends that your relationship with each other is your first priority, your basic relationship?

   1.

   2.

   3.

   4.

83

11 God's Goal for Your Marriage

As much as leaving and cleaving are essential for a real marriage, there is no marriage at all without the third element—"one flesh."

> For this cause a man shall leave his father and his mother, and shall cleave to his wife; and they shall become one flesh (Gen. 2:24).

Obviously, this applies to the physical union of husband and wife in marriage. Without it there is no real marriage. Through the physical union a man and woman become "one flesh."

Paul quotes our text in 1 Corinthians 6:16 to correct immoral conduct. Such a relationship is never a passing thing, an incidental thing, nor an innocent thing. It makes two people one.

Our text is quoted once again by Paul in Ephesians 5:31 as proof that the wife is part of the husband. Through their physical union she becomes part of him. This becomes, then, the basis for a husband's love for his wife. He is to love her as himself because she is part of him.

In the opinion of many students our text goes beyond the sexual union to an even deeper union in marriage. It is the total union of two persons—body, soul, and spirit—into one person.

"Ideally marriage is the submersion of two partial selves into the creation of one whole self" (Carlyle).

For the Christian couple, marriage should be

One new life existent in two persons! Here is equal dignity and worth and the recognition of the individual place of each; here is true oneness at every level of being and doing.[1]

This is the divine ideal. It is God's goal for your marriage. It begins with true intimacy in spirit. It overflows into the soul relationship. It is expressed and symbolized in the body relationship.

Much more remains to be said about this aspect of your marriage. It will be so much more appropriate and meaningful to reserve a discussion of the topic to the last section of this study guide.

Notes

[1]Dwight Small, *Design for Christian Marriage* (Westwood, New Jersey: Fleming H. Revell, 1959), p. 26.

12   Who's in Charge?

The success of a marriage depends not only on having the right partner, but on being the right partner.

—*Abraham Lincoln*

Being the right partner, for a Christian husband, involves three basic responsibilities. He is to lead his wife, love her, and honor her.

In this chapter we want to consider only the first: the leadership of the husband.

"What? You mean the husband is in charge?"

How do you read these verses?

. . . the husband is the head of the wife, as Christ also is the head of the church . . . (Eph. 5:23).

. . . the man is the head of a woman . . . (1 Cor. 11:3).

He must be one who manages his own household well . . . (1 Tim. 3:4).

The concept of leadership is derived from the metaphor of the human body. What the head is to the body, the husband is to the wife. What the body is without a head, a wife is without a true husband.

The significance of headship is immeasurably enhanced by the analogy of Christ and His church. What our Lord is to the church, the husband is to his wife. What the church is without Christ, a wife is without a Christian husband.

Headship implies three things: union, authority, and responsibility. The husband becomes the head of his wife by virtue of a vital union established at marriage. As of that moment he becomes an authority over her. With that authority he assumes total responsibility for her in every area of her being. To ignore any one of these three things is to distort and pervert headship. Each of these aspects warrants a closer look. Let me address myself to you, "the husband-to-be."

FIRST, AS HEAD, YOU WILL BE IN VITAL UNION WITH HER

What a marvelous mystery! The two become one (Gen. 2:24; Matt. 19:5). This will be confessed in your marriage vows. It will be symbolized in your physical relationship which consummates these vows. It will be expressed in the sharing of a common surname. You will become one. The union reaches to the very depths of your being. In a vital sense on every level of your existence you become one. The husband is as vitally united to the wife as the head is to the body. The wife is as much a part of the husband as the body is a part of the head. You will be one.

SECOND, AS HEAD, YOU WILL POSSESS AUTHORITY OVER HER

Inherent in the concept of headship is the principle of authority. To make such a statement today is almost as foolish as waving a red flag before a herd of charging bulls. At worst, it is tantamount to suicide. At best, it is chauvinistic. And yet, after having calculated the risks, this statement is unashamedly made. My only hope for survival lies in correcting the prevailing misrepresentations and misunderstandings.

Did you know that there are at least five kinds of "social power," authority or influence that human beings exercise over each other?[1]

Dr. Duane Litfin helpfully summarizes them:

> The first is called *information power*. A person, or source, exerts this sort of "power" over another when the information he controls influences the thinking or behavior of the recipient. *Referent power* exists when the recipient identifies with the source and desires to be like him. Thus the source influences the recipient by his example. *Coercive-reward power* exists when the recipient believes that the source can and will punish or reward his behavior. *Expert power* is the sort of influence that

accrues to the source by knowing more or being able to do something better than the recipient. *Positional power* exists when the recipient accepts a relationship in which the source is permitted or obliged, because of his position, to prescribe behaviors for the recipient, and the recipient is obliged to accept this influence.[2]

Dr. Litfin goes on to make three astute observations:

In examining the nature of the husband's authority over his wife as spelled out in the Bible, three crucial points emerge. First, of the five kinds of power or authority listed above, only the fifth—positional power—is designated by the New Testament as belonging to the husband; and even this type of "power" is not uniquely the husband's, for there are areas of authority over her husband that a wife holds by virtue of her position as well (see, e.g. 1 Cor. 7:4). Second, the other four types of authority are equally available to the husband and wife alike. Although it is probably true that coercive-reward power should seldom if ever be used by either marriage partner, the Bible clearly encourages the wife to exert several of the other types of power over her husband (e.g. the use of referent power in 1 Pet. 3:1–4, and the use of expert power in Prov. 31). Third, *the type of power delegated by God to the husband is the only one of the five that does not depend on some inherent superiority on the part of the one exerting the authority. Rather it depends solely on the position God has given the husband in the overall hierarchy of human society.* Thus the wife is urged to submit herself to her husband "as to the Lord" (Eph. 5:22), for her submissive attitude is to be in response not to any intrinsic superiority of her male partner but to the design of a sovereign God who has placed her in the submissive role.[3]

Finally, he applies his observations to both sides of one of the most highly combustible controversies of our day.

Such considerations ought to provide a much more balanced view of the "authority" of the husband. Those who favor the subjugation of the wife have clearly failed to grasp the fact that God has granted to the husband only a limited type of authority over his wife for the sake of the smooth functioning of the home, and that this authority is always to be exercised in understanding love (1 Pet. 3:7). Indeed, the example the husband is to emulate here is nothing less than the lofty one of Christ's selfless giving of Himself for His bride, the church (Eph. 5:25–30). Likewise, those who advocate the eradication of the biblical roles for husband and wife have seemingly also missed the balance point; otherwise, they would not continue to insist that submission inevitably implies inferiority.[4]

The focus of the Scriptures is upon the wife giving up the leadership to her husband (see Gen. 3:16 and Eph. 5:22–24).

The husband is never instructed to take the lead or be the head. You are the head. You are so constituted by God Himself. Your wife is instructed simply to acknowledge it.

Perhaps an analogy with the Christian life will help here. Have you ever been challenged to make Christ Lord of your life? How common in a Spiritual Life conference. Yet how wrong. He is Lord! (Acts 2:36).

As Christ has been constituted Lord by God, and believers are to acknowledge Him as such, so the husband has been designated head by our Lord and the wife is to recognize him as such and respect his authority!

This does not for a moment, however, absolve you of your responsibility.

THIRD, AS HEAD, YOU WILL HAVE A SOLEMN RESPONSIBILITY

As the God-ordained leader, you will be responsible to your Lord for the direction, welfare, and growth of your wife and family.

One qualification of every elder and every deacon is that he has assumed this responsibility and is discharging it effectively.

> He must be one who manages his own household well, keeping his children under control with all dignity (1 Tim. 3:4).

> Let deacons be husbands of only one wife, and good managers of their children and their own households (1 Tim. 3:12).

What a responsibility you assume in marriage! You become the head of a new family unit and are responsible for its welfare: socially, spiritually, educationally, financially, physically, and in every other way. As leader, the initiative is to be taken by you in goal setting, problem solving, and decision making. You are to set the pace for the spiritual life of your family. You are to be the model of Christian character. Headship involves responsibility!

Notes

[1]Barry E. Collins and Bertram H. Raven, "Group Structure: Attraction, Coalitions, Communication, and Power," in *Handbook of Social Psychology*, Gardner Lindzey and Elliot Aronson, eds., 5 vols. (Reading, MA: Addison Wesley, 1969), 4: 166–168.

[2]A. Duane Litfin, "A Biblical View of the Marital Roles: Seeking a Balance," *Bibliotheca Sacra*, Vol. 133, No. 532, Oct.–Dec., 1976, pp. 335–336.

[3]Ibid., p. 336.

[4]Ibid., p. 337.

Project Page

1. What are the qualities of a good leader? For an example, consider how Christ exercises His headship over the church.

2. Reflect upon the family leadership of several biblical characters and list their strength and/or weakness.

	Strength	Weakness
(a) Abraham Genesis 12:11–12; 13:1–13.		
(b) Isaac Genesis 26:6ff.; 24:67; 27.		

    (c) Jacob
        Genesis 28.

    (d) David
        2 Samuel 11:14–15.

    (e) Eli
        1 Samuel 2–3.

3. Now is the time to develop leadership—before marriage. In what ways are you now assuming leadership in your relationship?

4. What three things are implied in the husband's headship according to the chapter you have been studying?

   1.

   2.

   3.

13   The Supreme Sacrifice

In a premarital counseling session, a young couple was once asked to explain the dynamics of a wife's submission and a husband's love.

As is so often the case, the young lady was wisely silent. But her gallant groom-to-be came to her rescue with these startling words of wisdom! "I think it means that we are to love each other, and whenever we disagree, I am to give her a hug and a kiss, and then we do things my way."

Such shallowness will never stand the scrutiny of Scripture. Focus, for a moment, on God's charge to you as a husband.

Husbands, love your wives . . .

The critical word, of course, is "love." Few words are more abused, ambiguous, or devoid of meaning in our mid-twentieth century society. A brief investment in the study of this word will yield dividends that will enrich your marriage for life.

In the Greek language there are four verbs that contain the concept of love.

1. *Eraō*—   to love sexually, sensually, passionately. From this verb we have derived our English adjective, erotic, and our noun, eroticism. Interestingly, *eraō* is never used in the New Testament.

2. *Stergō*—   to love in a filial relationship, family love. This verb occurs in 2 Timothy 3:3 and Romans 1:31 to describe persons without "natural affections."

3. *Phileō*— to love emotionally, a feeling of love. As Jesus wept by the tomb of Lazarus the Jews said, "Behold how He *loved* him" (John 11:36).
4. *Agapaō*— This is the New Testament ethic. It is *agape* love.

Teacher, which is the great commandment in the Law? And He said to him, "You shall love the Lord your God with all your heart, and with all your soul, and with all your mind. This is the great and foremost commandment. And a second is like to it, You shall love your neighbor as yourself" (Matt. 22:36–39).

Several distinctives of agape love can now be isolated.

1. *Agape is volitional, not emotional.*

Richardson's *Theological Word Book* explains that *agapaō* "has neither the warmth of *phileō* nor the intensity of *eraō*." It refers to "the will rather than to emotion."[1]

Bishop Stephen Neill calls it "the steady directing of the human will towards the well-being of another."[2]

C. H. Dodd has pointed out that agape "is not primarily an emotion or affection, it is primarily an active determination of the will. That is why it can be commanded, as feelings cannot."[3]

Kierkegaard declares that to say love is a feeling or anything of that kind is an unchristian concept of love.[4]

Obviously agape is a matter of the will. It is commanded in Scripture. We are to love our enemies (Matt. 5:43–48), our neighbors (Matt. 22:38–39), and our wives (Eph. 5:25) with an agape love. You cannot command an emotional love, but you can command a volitional love.

2. *Agape love is an attitude, not a feeling.*

3. *Agape love is discerning, not sentimental.*

True love decides to seek the well-being of another. It discerns between what is harmful and helpful to the wife and decides to seek what is the best for her.

4. *Agape love is unselfish.*

It is a love that is nonreciprocal. In his book *Situation Ethics,* Joseph Fletcher points out three kinds of ethics:[5]

95

An egotistic ethic (erotic) says:

"My first and last consideration is myself." It uses and exploits people.

A mutualistic ethic (philic) says:

"I will give as long as I receive." This is the common dynamic of a friendship. This reflects many marriages. They are based upon a 50-50 contract.

An altruistic ethic (agapeic) says:

"I will give requiring nothing in return." This is true Christian love. Here is the basic responsibility of a Christian husband.

Rudolph Bultmann has said: "In reality that love which is based on emotions of sympathy or affection is self love, for it is a love of preference, of choice, and the standards of the preference and choice is the self."[6]

"Husbands love your wives":

Volitionally—a matter of the will
Discerningly—seeking their welfare
Unselfishly—requiring nothing in return

To enable you to grasp the implications of loving your wife, the Spirit of God presents the principle by means of two dramatic pictures in Ephesians 5.

The ANALOGY	As Christ loved the church.	As husbands love their own bodies.
The CHARACTERISTIC	This is a love that *gives*.	This is a love that *cares*.
The PRINCIPLE	The pattern is Christ's union with His church.	The basis is the husband's union with his wife.

A. THE PATTERN FOR YOUR LOVE (vv. 25–27)

No passage in all of Scripture is more overwhelming, humbling, and devastating to a man. It cannot be avoided nor ignored. No relief is found by fleeing to the Greek text, for it only increases the pressure. You are to love your wife "as Christ also loved the church and gave Himself up for her." What a standard!

From heaven He came and sought her,
To Be His holy bride;
With His own blood He bought her,
And for her life He died.

Here is the pattern.
He gave: What?—Himself
      For whom?—His church
      Why?—To sanctify her that He might present
      her to Himself holy and blameless (vv. 26–27).
Here is the pattern to follow: *it is a love that gives.*

Most husbands would readily admit to being willing to die for their wives if some catastrophic emergency called for such a supreme sacrifice. Do you see the error here? The Scriptures say nothing about being *willing* to give yourself up for a wife! As Christ gave Himself up so also you are to give yourself up. You are to lay your life at the feet of your wife and give your life up for her, seeking her interests, deciding to do what is in her highest interests.

Of Oliver Goldsmith it was said, "He gave away his life in handfuls." This ought to be true of every Christian husband. He gives away his life in handfuls for his wife. This gives rise to the determinative question you must ask before proposing marriage. It is this: "Am I prepared to give up my life for this girl?"

For you, marriage involves the supreme sacrifice: the giving up of your life for your wife.

Recently I chuckled over a "Blues Chaser" in our local newspaper. It read: "A man who thinks marriage is a 50-50 proposition doesn't understand one of two things—women or fractions."

But who says marriage is a 50-50 proposition? Not the Lord. According to the Scriptures, the husband is to give his life in a 100 percent commitment—expecting nothing in return. It is an unconditional love. Overwhelming, isn't it?

Often I have read Ephesians 5:26–27 wondering why the Spirit of God ever included these verses in a passage relating to the husband-wife relationship. They seemed like a digression from the main line of the apostle's thoughts. Only recently have I begun to see their import.

As Christ gave His life up to sanctify His church and bring

it to moral and spiritual perfection, so the husband is to give up his life to bring his wife to maturity in every level of her being. Here is the God-appointed purpose. Here is your responsibility as a husband to your wife. Here is an admirable goal for your marriage. Her personality, talents, spiritual gifts, and Christian character ought to be a major concern to you. Your role is to bring her to her full potential in every area.

The pattern for the husband's love, then, is Christ's love for His church. It is a love that gives. This kind of love will surely win a submissive wife. A page from ancient history makes just this point.

The wife of one of the generals of Cyrus, the ruler of Persia, was charged with treachery against the king and condemned to die. When her husband realized what had taken place, he ran to the palace and threw himself on the floor before the king. "O king, take my life instead of hers. Let me die in her place," he pleaded. Cyrus, who by all historical accounts was a noble and extremely sensitive man, was touched by this offer. "Love like that must not be spoiled by death," he said, and gave the husband and wife back to each other.

As they walked away, the husband said, "Did you notice how kindly the king looked upon us when he gave you the free pardon?" The wife replied, "I had no eyes for the king. I saw only the man who was willing to die in my place."

The husband who is willing to give up his life for his wife will surely win back a submissive wife for himself. Here are the dynamics of a Christian marriage relationship.

If in verses 25–27 we have the how of a Christian husband's love, in verses 28–33 we have the why.

B. THE BASIS FOR YOUR LOVE (vv. 28–33)

Why should you so love your wife? It is because she is part of you. God sees a married couple as an organism—the male and female of one entity.

Her union with you is—stated (v. 28)
　　　　　　　　　　　　—illustrated (vv. 29–30)
　　　　　　　　　　　　—symbolized (v. 31)

It is because she is part of you that you are to love her.

This adds another dimension to your love. It is not only to be a love that gives (vv. 25–27) but also *it is a love that cares* (vv. 28–31).

There are two words in our text that indicate how the husband ought to care for his wife—"nourish" and "cherish" (v. 29).

	NOURISH	CHERISH
Meaning	To rear, feed	To warm, to heat, to cuddle
Usage	Genesis 45:11—fed in Egypt Ephesians 5:4—bringing up children	Deuteronomy 22:6—bird on a nest 1 Thessalonians 2:7—care for children
Application	Material needs Spiritual needs	Emotional needs

Several years ago I heard someone describe the seven ages of a marriage cold.

1st year   "Sugar dumpling—I am worried about my baby girl. You must have a few days in the hospital to get rid of that cold. I don't expect you to eat that terrible hospital food so I'm having your food sent up from Howard Johnson's."

2nd year   "Listen darling, I don't like the sound of that cough, you be a good girl and go to bed for papa. I'll see that everything is looked after."

3rd year   "Come sweetheart, maybe you had better lie down. I'll bring you something to eat."

4th year   "Look dear, after you feed the kids and get the dishes washed, you'd better hit the sack."

5th year   "Get yourself a couple of aspirins."

6th year   "If you would just gargle or something and stop sitting around barking."

7th year   "For Pete's sake, stop sneezing. Do you want to give me pneumonia?"

This will never be the case in a truly Christian marriage. A Christian husband will love his wife with a love that unselfishly gives and genuinely cares.

Why did Paul say, *"Husbands,"* love your wives. . . ? Is there not supposed to be a mutual love? Why, then, did Paul not exhort the wives to love their husbands? After all, we are to "love one another."

Dr. Gene Getz answers:

> First, it is God's ordained plan for a man to be a Christlike leader in the home.
>
> Second, to love as Christ loved is the most difficult thing for a man to do, especially in a culture where women were often treated like slaves. Thus Paul emphasized this in the Ephesian and Colossian letters.
>
> Third, when a man loves as Christ loved, it produces the best results in his own life, in his wife's life, and in the life of his family.
>
> Fourth, and again most important, when a man sets the example of loving his wife as Christ loved, it will permeate the whole family, creating unity and harmony, which in turn becomes the most basic ingredient in being a witness to the non-Christian world.[7]

Husband—love your wife!

Notes

[1]C. E. B. Cranfield, "Love," *Theological Word Book of the Bible* (London: SCM Press, Ltd., 1951), pp. 131–136.

[2]Quoted by F. D. Croggan, *The New Testament Basis of Moral Theology* (London: Tyndale Press, 1948), p. 8.

[3]C. H. Dodd, *Gospel and Law* (New York: Columbia University Press, 1951), p. 42.

[4]S. A. Kierkegaard, *The Journals* translated by Alexander Dru (London: Oxford University Press, 1938), entry 932, p. 317.

[5]Joseph Fletcher, *Situation Ethics* (Philadelphia: The Westminster Press, 1966), p. 109.

[6]Rudolf Bultmann, *Jesus and the Word* (New York: Charles Scribner's Sons, 1958), p. 117.

[7]Gene A. Getz, *The Measure of a Family* (Glendale, California: Regal Books Division, Gospel Light Publications, 1976), pp. 33–34.

Project Page

1. Do you recall the two similes in Ephesians 5:25–33? The husband is to love his wife "as":

   1. _____(vv. 25–27).
   2. _____(vv. 28–33).

   Which is the basis for loving your wife? _____

   Which is your pattern? _____

2. Describe *agape* love in your own words.

3. Why do you suppose the wife is never instructed so to love her husband?

4. In what ways can you begin now to "nourish" your fiancée?

5. Colossians 3:19 adds a further dimension to the Ephesians 5 passage. Read it carefully. What causes the wife to become bitter against her husband now?

How is her bitterness cured?

How can this kind of bitterness be prevented?

6. The directive given in Ephesians 5:32 is the fourth occurrence of these very words in Scripture (Gen. 2:24; Matt. 19:5; Mark 10:7). Each time it starts with the phrase "For this cause. . . ." What "cause" is understood?

14   Life's Greatest Challenge

Several years ago I was invited to speak at a weekend men's retreat in southern Texas. The campgrounds were nestled in the midst of some of the most beautiful terrain in the world. What a weekend it was. Hearts were challenged and lives were changed as God, by His Spirit, took our text and graciously burned it into our beings. Each session focused upon this verse. We came at it from every direction. Gradually it opened up before us in all of its delightful and dazzling beauty, with all of its profound and revolutionizing truth.

I had been married for almost twenty years. Not until that weekend, however, did I come to grips with the issues of this text. It has become to me, as a husband, the single most significant verse in all of Scripture. Its precious contents make it a valuable gem. Its shattering implications make it an explosive time bomb. Handle it with care!

Here it is.

> You husbands likewise, live with your wives in an understanding way, as with a weaker vessel, since she is a woman; and grant her honor as a fellow-heir of the grace of life, so that your prayers may not be hindered (1 Peter 3:7).

For every Christian husband there is a double responsibility woven into this text. Each responsibility is tied into the recognition of a rather obvious fact and is based on a very significant reason.

It may be stated as follows:

	OUR ACTIONS	OUR ATTITUDE
Our RESPONSIBILITY	Live with your wife in an understanding way	Grant her honor
Our RECOGNITION	As a weaker vessel	As a fellow-heir of the grace of life
Our REASON	Since she is a Woman	So your prayers may not be hindered

According to this verse your wife is to be four things to you.

FIRST, SHE IS TO BE THE OBJECT OF YOUR MOST DILIGENT AND CAREFUL STUDY

You are to live together with her in an understanding way. The verb Peter uses in the original text underlines the idea of togetherness. You are not just to dwell in the same house with her. You are "to live together" with her. A Christian husband does not just live with his wife. He "lives together" with her. And that means that you are to live with her in view of your understanding of her. That's right. A little jolting, isn't it? The husband is to live with his wife according to his knowledge of her temperament and personality and constitution.

Many a gallant groom launches his marriage with a crusade to correct his bride. Secretly in his mind he has isolated those two or three things that must go as soon as they are married. More unrealistically still, he has convinced himself that those several areas that are problems before their marriage (moodiness, oversensitivity, bossiness) will disappear when she gets away from home. Most dangerous of all, he looks upon his bride-to-be as a horse trainer looks upon a colt—a real challenge, a young lady who needs to be trained to live with him.

Such a marriage is set on a stormy course. You are to live

with your wife according to your understanding of her needs, personality, interests, and temperament.

Every wife is a distinctive creation. Your wife will be different than your mother, your aunt, and even your best friend's wife. It is of the highest priority that you take time to get to know her well and understand her thoroughly. This is a husband's greatest challenge in life. Above all others, he is to know and understand his wife. What makes her tick? What turns her off? What turns her on? What does she need? How must she be treated when she is tired, lonely, or anxious? There it is—life's greatest challenge!

She must become the object of your most careful and diligent study. You must study her more carefully than a broker studies his stock market, or a football coach studies his athletes, or a scientist studies his research animals. Then, in view of your observations, live with her accordingly.

Some wives can be teased, others can't. Some can adjust to frequent moves, others can't. One requires more listening time than another. Your wife may not be able to cope with unexpected supper guests while your associate's wife can. Many wives need eight hours of sleep, a few need six. Some are late nighters and late risers, others are early to bed and early to rise. The husband is to live with his wife according to his knowledge of her personality and needs!

SECOND, SHE IS YOUR WEAKER VESSEL

> The weaker sex is understood
> To mean the whole of womanhood;
> But I have yet to find a man
> Who knows whom it is weaker than.
> —*Anonymous*

Nevertheless, as a general rule, the woman is the weaker vessel. Someone has well said that a woman is like a finely-made delicate but durable watch. Emotionally and physically she is a delicate creature. Recognizing your wife as such a creative work of God will encourage you to live with her in an understanding way. Caring for her, and living together with her requires a delicate, sensitive touch.

Such a husband is a rare breed. Why is it so difficult to do? Why is it so seldom done? The casualty rate here is astronomical. Scores of disastrous and tempestuous marriages could find security and tranquillity if the husband would but live with his wife in an understanding way. What is the secret to such a course of action? It is a matter of attitude! This brings us to the third thing she is to you.

THIRD, SHE IS THE MOST PRECIOUS POSSESION GOD HAS GIVEN YOU ON EARTH

If the first half of our text focuses upon your action as a husband, the second half points to your attitude. Observe carefully the cause-effect relationship between these two parts of the verse.

The Effect	The Cause
YOUR ACTIONS live in an understanding way	YOUR ATTITUDE grant her honor

One is the fruit, the other the root. The husband who does not honor his wife will never seek to understand her in order to live with her in an understanding way. The key is your attitude toward her. You are to grant her honor. As the child is to honor his parents (Eph. 6:2), so the husband is to honor his wife.

To honor a wife is to regard her as a person of great value. It is to esteem her highly. She is to be considered the most precious "object" you will ever possess.

In our home we have two sets of dishes. The plastic ones are used by one and all on any occasion. We put them in the dishwasher and expose them to all kinds of hazards. Not so with our good china dishes. Our young children seldom touch them. They are always washed by hand. We reserve them for very special occasions. We regard them as objects of great value (our attitude) and treat them accordingly (our action)!

So it is with the husband and wife. The root problem so often is a matter of attitude. You are to grant her honor, regard her as a person of great worth and value. The recognition that she is a fellow-heir of the gracious gift of life will help you here. She is not an animal with a life that is lower than mankind. She is a being possessing human life, having been created in the image of God. The distinctiveness of human life in Genesis 3 becomes the basis for the sanctity of human life in Genesis 9. As you are, so is your fiancée. Both are heirs of the gracious gift of human life. You are to grant her honor, esteem her highly, as a creature made in the image of God. God loves her and honors her. He has given her eternal life, His life as well.

FINALLY, SHE IS A KEY TO YOUR PRAYER LIFE

Someone has well said that God will not even hear the prayers of the man who is too ignorant to know how to treat his wife, or too foolish to value her as the greatest gift God has for him on earth.

Our text, however, may go beyond this. It may be speaking of something other than God hearing our prayers. Many husbands and wives find it very difficult to pray together. Either they have never tried it, or they have been embarrassed when they did try. Could the problem be traced back to the very issue of our text? I believe this is often the case. It's a problem of attitude. The husband who does not regard his wife highly, who does not set a great value on her, will seldom seek the solitude of the secret place of prayer with her.

Grant her honor! This may involve carrying out the garbage for her every morning. It requires speaking to her respectfully, politely, kindly. It prohibits purposely doing things that will provoke or disturb her. It calls for adjustments on your part—not hers. Perhaps above all, it means being courteous and considerate.

Billy Graham makes the point with a before-and-after scene. Before marriage, he suggests, the young suitor opens the car door for his date, extends a hand, and says, "Darling, won't you step out." He even parks the car to avoid puddles. After marriage he parks in the midst of a puddle and, as he leaps from his side, he shouts, "Jump honey, I think you can make it!"

Could this be a Christian husband?

Project Page

1. List five distinctives of your fiancée that will require particular understanding in your marriage.

    1.

    2.

    3.

    4.

    5.

2. Now is the time to begin to grant her honor. List five specific ways you will give honor to her, beginning now.

    1.

2.

3.

4.

5.

3. How would you rate the level of your understanding of your fiancée?

    1. Needs no improvement
    2. Highly effective
    3. Satisfactory
    4. Inconsistent
    5. Superficial
    6. Frustrating
    7. Highly inadequate

    How would your fiancée describe your understanding of her?

4. What are the three basic responsibilities that are yours as a Christian husband?

    1.

    2.

    3.

5. Memorize: Ephesians 5:25; 1 Peter 3:7.

6. Now you are ready to interact with one of the toughest issues of our day. According to Ephesians 5:21, we are to "be subject to one another in the fear of Christ." Generally, this injunction is applied to the wife and reserved for her role in marriage (see Eph. 5:22). However, verse 21 seems to imply that submitting to one another is a two-way street, even in a marriage. More will be said about the wife's submission to her husband in a later chapter. But what about a husband's submission to his wife?

    a) Does Ephesians 5:21 apply to the Christian husband in his relationship with his wife?

b) How will you reconcile the principle of submission and headship in your role as husband?

c) In view of the content of these last three chapters, illustrate, specifically, ways in which you should and will be submissive to your wife!

7. What questions on the role of the husband need to be raised and explored in your next counseling session?

15 Help Is On the Way

When William Jennings Bryan went to call on the father of his prospective wife to seek the hand of his daughter in marriage, knowing the strong religious feelings of the father, he thought he would strengthen his case by a quotation from the Bible. He quoted the proverb of Solomon: "Whoso findeth a wife findeth a good thing" (Prov. 18:22).

But to his surprise, the father replied with a citation from Paul to the effect that he who marries does well, but he who does not marry does better!

The young suitor was for a moment confounded. Then with a happy inspiration he replied that Paul had no wife and Solomon had seven hundred. Solomon, therefore, ought to be the better judge as to marriage![1]

Dubious as his interpretation was, who will contest the wisdom of Solomon: "Whoso findeth a wife findeth a good thing"—especially, if she is a Christian wife?

There is no more attractive creature on earth than a truly Christian wife. When bachelor George Whitefield visited New England, he was invited to the house of Jonathan Edwards. While there, he was greatly impressed with the loveliness of Mrs. Edwards and the felicity of their home life.

In his diary he wrote: "She is a woman adorned with a meek and quiet spirit and talked so feelingly and so solidly of the things of God, and seemed to be such a helpmeet to her husband, that she caused me to renew those prayers which for some months I have put up to God, that He would send a daughter of Abraham to be my wife."[2]

A Christian wife is far more than a wife who is a

Christian. Let me speak directly to you who are about to assume this prestigious role and say that first, you will be your husband's helper.

> Then the Lord God said, "It is not good for the man to be alone; I will make him a helper suitable for him" (Gen. 2:18).

Eve was Adam's helper. So also was Sarah to Abraham, Rachel to Jacob, Ruth to Boaz, Priscilla to Aquila.

A. SPIRITUALLY

There is no doubt in my mind that the greatest influence on my life has been the example, counsel, and instruction of my parents. They had, of course, an advantage over others. Their input was during the most formative years of my life. When I was a young tender plant my mother and father nurtured, directed, and corrected me. When I was a handful of clay, they molded my character and shaped my value system. Today, I joyfully and honestly rise up and call them "blessed!"

There is no less doubt in my mind, that my wife, Marilyn, stands second in line. What an influence she has had on my personal and public life. In every sense of the word, she has been my helper.

I suppose I appreciate her most for the spiritual help she has been to me. In each of the major decisions of our married life she has faithfully and earnestly wrestled with God in prayer both by herself and by my side. In the process of decision making, she has offered an objective point of view that has invariably worked to bring my perspective into balance. When we have settled together on what we believe to be the will of God, she has never looked back, only forward, to support and to help.

Our decision, twelve years ago, to move to Texas and attend seminary was a big one! It meant selling all our earthly possessions, leaving family and friends, settling in a place where we did not know one soul, living at a poverty level, and investing countless hours in the books. In my most objective moments of reflection, such a move, at my age, with three children, seemed outrageous. When my faith wavered, when my commitment sputtered almost to the point of stalling, my wife came to the rescue. Without her faith, vision, willingness to sacrifice, and immense encouragement we never would have taken the first step. Before God I can say that without her standing by my side we would never have finished the course.

For twenty years she has been a patient listener and constructive critic of my sermons. As a "sounding board" for illustrations and applications she has been both sensitive and perceptive. Often, I have changed my notes or eliminated a point as a result of her input.

Her greatest contribution to my spiritual life has come in the area of reading. Not only does she read much more quickly than I do, but also much more widely. She loves to read autobiographies, biographies, and historical novels. The Reformation period and the Great Awakening have a particular attraction to her. She reads secular periodicals on current social and political issues. She devours missionary books of the finest quality. Frankly, I do not have the time for such reading, but profit tremendously from her in these areas. Marilyn clips illustrations for sermons, points out articles that I need to read, and condenses books as "small talk" when we sit or drive together. She sifts the material and nourishes me with the best. She separates the milk and feeds me the cream.

B. Emotionally

When God brings a husband and wife together He designs the relationship so that each will be an emotional helper to the other. For this to be functional the spouse, of necessity, must be cut from different emotional patterns. Then, and only then, can the one "help" the other.

What a helper my wife has been in this area of our married life. She tempers my drive and intensity; she balances my impulsiveness and hardness; she adds compassion and grace to my less attractive tendencies. She is the epitome of patience—a quality sadly lacking in her husband. The Lord knew exactly what I needed, and He gave me Marilyn. I would be less than honest if I said I always appreciate it. Yet, I do see His wisdom in it all. Often we have laughed together at the monstrous marriage that would have resulted if her emotional make-up was similar to mine.

She encourages me when I am discouraged. She supports me when I am staggering. She motivates me to keep going on when I want to stop. She listens, understands, and helps when despair knocks at the door of my life.

C. SOCIALLY

Although I did not know it when we married, I now realize that Marilyn has the gift of hospitality. She enjoys entertaining and is unselfish with her home. Over the years she has developed organizational skills that have transformed pressure-packed crisis-riddled evenings into relaxed and delightful experiences. Often such an event is the spiritual "high" of our week. As I reflect on our marriage and ministry, in our home and out of our home, I would have to acknowledge that any accurate assessment of her help to me, socially, is impossible. To estimate it generally, it has been immense, undoubtedly even greater than I imagine.

Just to set the record straight, you need to know that Marilyn is far more than a helper to me. She has a life of her own which is both full and fruitful. As a joke last Christmas, I bought her a kitchen apron which read: "I'd rather play tennis." At least I thought it was funny. She does play tennis and loves it. It has been a wonderful opportunity to meet ladies in our community and build evangelistic bridges. She also plays paddle-tennis in a local club, paints as a hobby, works at several different crafts, sews, and entertains groups of ladies. Her personal counseling and public teaching ministries are expanding to ladies' retreats and Christian women's clubs. The latest addition has been an exciting discipleship class with three ladies from our church fellowship. Even with all of this, she continues to be my helper.

According to the Word of God, the purpose for Eve's creation is clear. She was to help Adam. This was the basic reason for her being. She was not to be his servant or slave, but she was to be a helper. She was made to be his complement. She was created for man (1 Cor. 11:9). This is a strategic and significant aspect of the biblical role for every Christian wife.

Notes

[1]Clarence Edward Macartney, *Macartney's Illustrations* (New York: Abingdon, 1965), p. 224.

[2]Quoted by J. Vernon Jacobs, *450 True Stories From Church History* (Grand Rapids: Eerdmans, 1955), p. 130.

Project Page

Think creatively, individually, critically.
In what specific ways can you be your husband's helper?

1. Spiritually

2. Emotionally

3. Socially

4. Intellectually

16 An Explosive Issue

No issue is more explosive today than the matter of submission. Yet, as a biblical principle, it could not be clearer. It exists in four spheres:

In the state	citizens to government	Romans 13:1 Titus 3:1
In the world	slaves to masters	Titus 2:9
In the church	members to elders members to one another members to Christ	1 Peter 5:5 Ephesians 5:21 Ephesians 5:24
In the home	children to parents wives to husbands husbands to Christ	Ephesians 6:1–2 Ephesians 5:22 1 Corinthians 11:3

Our society today is marked by unrest and instability in all four spheres. There is no doubt that one of the major contributing factors is the prevailing spirit of rebellion. And yet, to mention the matter of submission in most circles is to ignite an exceedingly short fuse.

But we cannot avoid it. As a Christian wife, you will be a subordinate in rank.

Wives, be subject to your own husbands . . . (Eph. 5:22).

Wives, be subject to your husbands . . . (Col. 3:18).

. . . the man is the head of a woman . . . (1 Cor. 11:3).

. . . being subject to their own husbands . . . (Titus 2:3–5).

. . . you wives, be submissive to your own husbands . . . (1 Peter 3:1).

I think I understand why the question of submission is currently such an explosive issue. Most husbands have misused their authority, many wives have misunderstood their roles, and far too many preachers have misrepresented this principle.

Mrs. Martha Montgomery in her series on "The Godly Woman" gives us a helpful comparison of three related terms.

When the woman was in her unfallen state God appointed her to be *subordinate* to the man (Gen. 2:18). This was a matter of rank and did not imply any inferiority. It was an honorable position.

So we see, first, a *woman* is a *subordinate*.

This is a matter of *rank*.

It is by God's *appointment*.

After the woman had sinned, in her fallen state, God imposed subjection on her (Gen. 3:16).

So second, a *woman* is in *subjection*.

This is the matter of her husband's *rule*.

It is *imposed* by God.

In the New Testament the wife is enjoined to come into submission (Eph. 5:22–24) to her husband.

Third, a *woman* is to be *submissive*.

This is a matter of *inner attitude*.

It is to be *voluntarily assumed*.

The inner attitude is toward the subordination appointed and the subjection imposed in Genesis.

In extrabiblical Greek it was primarily a military term that denoted a rank under another.[1] Literally the verb means "to arrange or to rank under." The word implies a rank subordinate to one who is in authority, to whom obedience and respect are due.

It does not imply any inferiority of person but only subordination in rank. As a person you will be no more inferior to your husband, than the citizen is to his government or Christ is to God. Yet, the citizen is subordinate in rank to the governor. Christ in His humanity was subordinate to God the Father. You are to assume volitionally and voluntarily a rank or office under your husband in the administration of your home and family.

It does not justify suppression by your husband but does imply obedience to your husband. Submission does not stifle your leadership, creativity, and initiative as a wife. You may well wonder if it implies that you will make no decisions, offer no argument, participate in no discussions. Absolutely not. What a vanilla wife you would be! What kind of a helper is this? It is not only your right but also your responsibility to function as a partner in this partnership. Every Christian husband should consult his wife as his closest advisor and make decisions with her interests in view. Often responsibilities will be delegated to you requiring important decisions that must be made by you. And yet, when your husband makes decisions, you are responsible to obey. That is submission.

Some of us know wives who do obey but are not truly submissive. A third implication in our New Testament word is that of respect for your husband in his position and for his decisions. A wife who obeys without respect is not in submission. You are to "reverence" ("fear," Eph. 5:33, same word as in v. 21) your husband. The church's reverence for Christ is your pattern. You may not agree with the decision or even respect him as a person, but you are to respect him in his position as head. The mother who enforces her husband's rules or disciplines, but lets her children know she does not agree, is not respecting her husband before her children. Such lack of respect is most often seen in the use of the tongue. Beware!

Such an injunction from the early apostles was much needed in the church of the first century.

In his commentary on Ephesians, Eadie has said;

> In those days wives when converted and elevated from comparative servitude might be tempted, in the novel consciousness of freedom, to encroach a little as if to put to the test the extent of their recent liberty and enlargement.[2]

Is such an injunction any less needed today? Why does

God say: *"Wives,* be subject to your husbands"? Hear again
Dr. Gene Getz:

> First, it is God's ordained plan that a woman should not domi-
> nate or control her husband. And the opposite was becoming a
> trend in the pagan world, particularly in the vicinity of Ephesus.
> Second, submitting is one of the most difficult things for many
> wives to do. Ever since sin entered the world it is a natural
> tendency for all human beings to resist authority. In fact, sin
> entered the world due to disobedience and an unwillingness to
> submit to God's authority. Thus Paul is treating a universal prob-
> lem.
> Third, when women violate this psychological law they will
> inevitably experience increased unhappiness and insecurity. On
> the other hand, when a woman conforms to this law, it produces
> the best results for her personally, it ministers in a significant way
> to her husband, and it creates special benefits for the family.
> Fourth, and most important, when a woman does fulfill her
> God-ordained role, she is helping create an environment that
> will contribute significantly to helping her family become an
> outstanding testimony to the non-Christian world. In short, she is
> helping to carry out the Great Commission.[3]

The central passage on our subject is Ephesians 5:22–24.
Let us dissect it carefully to examine the various facets of
your role.

A. THE SPHERE OF YOUR SUBMISSION

It is to your *"own"* husband (v. 22). This is an intensive
possessive pronoun. It emphasizes the intimacy of the marriage union—your *own* husband. It stresses the exclusive-
ness of that union—*your* own husband.

In the thinking of the New Testament writers this must be
a very crucial point. The word occurs in 1 Peter 3:1, 5 and
Titus 2:5, as well as Ephesians 5:22.

Submission in a Christian marriage is to the one man
whom God has given to you for your own. Paul, knowing
this would be a difficult task, continues with a word that
helps.

B. THE MOTIVATION FOR YOUR SUBMISSION

It is to be done "as to the Lord" (v. 22). Not to Christ, but
to the Lord! His lordship is in view. You are to submit as to

your master—your Lord, Jesus Christ. You are to submit to your husband, rendering it as a service to your Lord.

What could be more transforming to any marriage than such an attitude? Obvious to all, your relationship to your Lord will be clearly reflected in your relationship to your husband. A rebellious wife is telegraphing to all her rebelliousness against the Lord. Her obedience to her husband is part of her obedience to her Lord. One is part of the other.

C. THE BASIS FOR YOUR SUBMISSION

It is because "the husband is the head of the wife" (Eph. 5:23).

This will be news to many husbands. The experience of some is expressed by an anonymous poet who writes:

> A woman may be small of frame
> With tiny feet that patter.
> But when she puts one small foot down
> Her shoe size doesn't matter.

Yet God has constituted the husband as head. This is clearly taught in the Scriptures (1 Cor. 11:3, 8–9; 1 Tim. 2:11–14). His headship is analogous to Christ's headship in the church. Two heads in the church are just as unthinkable as two queen bees in a hive. Division would be inevitable. So also in a marriage.

No head in the church would be as intolerable as an army without a general or a country without a president. Chaos, disorder, anarchy would follow. So also in marriage.

A usurping head, a person who takes the headship unlawfully in the church, would be blasphemous. It would lead to nothing but confusion. So also in marriage.

The analogy with the church, and the metaphor of the human body, teach us that three important elements are implied in headship:

—union with the wife
—authority over the wife
—responsibility for the wife

This position is given to your husband by the Lord. Here is the basis for a Christian wife's submission to her husband.

The relationship between Christ and His church provides

a pattern not only for the headship of the husband but also for the submission of the wife. This brings us to the standard for your submission.

D. The Standard for Your Submission

It is "as the church is subject to Christ" (Eph 5:24). What a standard!

The church is subject to Christ voluntarily, wholeheartedly, enthusiastically, sincerely. Here is the pattern for every Christian wife.

What a sermon this role will preach to the world around you. What an object lesson for your children to behold. You have the opportunity and privilege of presenting to all a real life example of the church's attitude toward her Lord and Head.

E. The Extent of Your Submission

It is "in everything" (v. 24). The Lord calls for an absolute and total submission. In Ephesians 5 Christian marriage is in view. A Christian husband surely would never order his wife to do anything contrary to the Scriptures. In a Christian marriage the wife should never have to face the conflict with her higher obligation to obey God. In this kind of marriage, therefore, submission is absolute—"in everything."

Such submission is never easy. How is it ever to be achieved?

F. The Enablement for Your Submission

It is by means of the Holy Spirit.

Have you noted the cause-effect relationship between the preceding paragraph and the instruction to the Christian wife in verses 22–24?

Ephesians 5:18–21	Ephesians 5:22–24
Filling of Holy Spirit	Role of Wife
Results: —praise —thanksgiving —mutual submission	Responsibility: —submission to her husband

The filling of the Spirit results in praise, thanksgiving, and submission. The last of these becomes the theme of verses 22–24. The wife's submission is not the product of personality, time, or maturity. It is the product of a spiritual life controlled by the Spirit of God.

As a result, your own personal spiritual development becomes a high priority. Your intake and assimilation of the Word of God, your prayer life, your communion with Christ, is the spring from which will flow a submissive spirit.

G. THE ENCOURAGEMENT FOR YOUR SUBMISSION

It is your husband's love for you.

It would be nothing less than criminal to leave Ephesians 5:22–24 without observing the cause-effect relationship with the paragraph that follows. In 5:25–33 the role of the husband is set forth. Simply, he is to love his wife as Christ loved the church. He is to give up his life to and for his wife. What an encouragement toward submission!

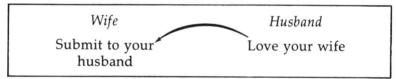

Wife	*Husband*
Submit to your husband	Love your wife

What Christian wife will find it difficult to submit to a man who is constantly giving up his life for her?

Your submission is:

divinely established from above—God
humanly encouraged from without—husband
ultimately enabled from within—Holy Spirit

It seems to me that the most effective way to defuse the explosive issue of submission is to see it neatly nestled between the principle of mutual submission (5:21) and the practice of a husband's love (5:25–33). This puts it in proper perspective and elevates it to an honorable and spiritual level.

Notes

[1]W. E. Vine, *An Expository Dictionary of New Testament Words* (London: Oliphants, 1953), IV, 86.

[2]John Eadie, *A Commentary on the Epistle of Paul to the Ephesians* (London: Griffin, Bohn and Company, 1861), p. 417.

[3]Gene Getz, *The Measure of a Family* (Glendale, California: Regal Books, 1976), pp. 32–33.

Project Page

1. Make a list of at least twenty specific areas that will be included "in everything" (Eph. 5:24) in your marriage.

2. Which will be the most difficult for you? Why? How do you plan to resolve it?

3. What should be your plan of action when you think your husband has made a wrong decision? Consider: Ephesians 4:29; Proverbs 21:1; Ephesians 6:18; 1 Thessalonians 5:18; Ephesians 5:24.

4. Now for a review:

   a. What is the sphere of your submission?
   b. What is the motivation?
   c. What is the basis?
   d. Can you recall the standard?
   e. What is the extent?
   f. Where is the enablement?
   g. Where should you look for encouragement?

5. We have suggested that the husband's love for his wife (5:25–33) may be a cause producing the effect of encouraging the wife's submission to her husband (5:22–24). Could the cause-effect relationship work the other way too? In what sense might 5:22–24 be a cause producing the effect of 5:25–33?

6. Give your personal evaluation of the two following quotations:

   a. "Submission removes the freedom of a wife."

   b. "No competent theologian today takes the Pauline statements about women as prescriptive for the twentieth century."

7. Suppose your husband does not lead spiritually. What is your responsibility to the Lord?

17 Your Highest Vocation

American families are in trouble—trouble so deep and so perva-
sive as to threaten the future of our nation.[1]

This is the considered opinion of a national perodical in
its major report on a White House Conference on Children.
The columnist went on to estimate that a half-million teen-
agers run away from home each year! Why? What is the
answer?

Dr. Loentine Young, noted child-care expert and execu-
tive director of the Child Service Association, elaborates on
the problem of fractured families.

Since the Second World War, mobility has become a way of life,
and the community has been destroyed. Relatives have been
separated with no thought of future reunion. Divorces have become common. Children have come to be regarded as economic
liabilities. Now we have the family with conflicting values, with
no clear indication of what ought to be done, and with no con-
sistent supports. You have family life in which everyone goes in
different directions: papa goes one way, mama goes another, and
the children go someplace else.[2]

But what is the solution? What is needed? Try these words
for size. Do they or do they not fit the problem?

Older women likewise are to be reverent in their behavior, not
malicious gossips, not enslaved to much wine, teaching what is
good, that they may encourage the young women to love their
husbands, to love their children, to be sensible, pure, workers at
home, kind, being subject to their own husbands, that the word
of God may not be dishonored (Titus 2:3–5).

129

Here is the third dimension to your role as a Christian wife. You will not only be your husband's helper, and his subordinate in rank, but,

YOU WILL BE THE HOMEMAKER

"A woman's place is in the home." True or False? The woman's place *is* in the home—primarily, but not exclusively. Let me explain.

As I understand it at least, the Bible does teach that the primary responsibility of a married woman is her home. Being a wife and mother is her highest priority on earth. I agree with Dr. Getz when he says: "If she neglects these priorities in order to develop a professional career or to accumulate material wealth, she is violating the direct teachings of scripture."[3] (See Gen. 2:18–24; Prov. 31:10–31; Titus 2:3–5.)

Tucked away in my files is a Peter Marshall quotation which I picked up sometime, somewhere. Everyone certainly will not agree with the initial point. However, the remainder of the statement is priceless for pointing out the multifaceted challenge before a homemaker.

> Modern girls argue that they have to earn an income in order to esablish a home which would be impossible on their husband's income. That is sometimes the case but it must always be viewed as a regrettable necessity, never as a natural thing for the wife to do. The average woman, if she gives her full time to her home, her husband, her children. . . . If she tries to understand her husband's work . . . to curb his egotism while at the same time building up his self esteem, to kill his masculine conceit while encouraging all his hopes, to establish around the family a circle of true friends. . . . If she provides in the home a proper atmosphere of culture, a love of music, of beautiful furniture and a garden. . . . If she will do all this she will be engaged in a life work that will demand every ounce of her strength, every bit of her patience, every talent God has given her, the utmost sacrifice of her love. It will demand everything that she has and more and she will find that for which she was created. She will know that she is carrying out the plan of God.

A homemaker—what an honored profession! What a high calling! What an overwhelming challenge!

And yet to say that a wife is exclusively a homemaker is to go beyond Scripture. As you will discover in your inductive study of the excellent wife (Prov. 31:10–31), your role may extend far beyond your home. There is room for an aggressive and successful business career in the life of an excellent wife. Some wives cannot cope with the spare time, the boredom, and the isolation of a home. They have abounding energy, particular skills or interest, and powerful drives, none of which are sufficiently challenged nor exhausted in the home. They need a secular job for their own sense of fulfillment. As a result they will invariably be more pleasant, entertaining, and interesting wives. They will bring into their homes a constant flow of new ideas, questions, and friends. Their input will be both varied and valued.

Each case must be considered on its own merits. The number of children, the ages of the children, the health of your husband, the stage of your married life, and a dozen other factors may well be considered.

Do you plan to be a working wife, that is, working outside your home? In discussing the subject, in making a decision:

> consider carefully your husband's request (Eph. 5:22–24).

> examine prayerfully your motives (2 Cor. 5:9).

> remember constantly your priority (Titus 2:3–5).

Notes

[1] *Time*, "The American Family: Future Uncertain" (Dec. 28, 1970), p. 34.

[2] *U. S. Catholic,* July, 1973.

[3] Gene Getz, *The Measure of a Family* (Glendale, California: Regal Books, 1976), p. 51.

Project Page

1. Reread and study carefully Titus 2:3–5. Here is a guide for homemakers. List the characteristics you see present in these verses.

   A radio station some time ago created a small tidal wave with a simple contest. The question they asked was this, "How can a wife keep her husband satisfied?"

   A woman who won the prize submitted an answer of only three words—"Feed the brute." Such an answer falls far short of meeting any biblical standards. As a Christian wife, you will have three basic responsibilities:

   Be a helper to your husband
   Be a subordinate of your husband
   Be a homemaker for your husband

   This produces satisfied husbands!

2. What question on the subject would you like to discuss in your counseling session?

Projects for Next Month

1. Complete Part Three of your study guide.

2. Read: Jay Adams, *Christian Living in the Home*, chapter 3. Also, pp. 77–84.

3. Highly recommended for extra reading:
   For the fiancé—Fred Renich, *The Christian Husband* (Wheaton: Tyndale, 1978), p. 249.

   For the fiancée—Elisabeth Elliott, *Let Me Be a Woman,* (Wheaton: Tyndale, 1978), p. 190.

Part Three

**Before
Your Marriage**

18 Frustration or Fulfillment

There are two kinds of people at parties—those who want to go home early and those who want to be the last ones to leave. The trouble is that they're usually married to each other!

Some time ago I read of a couple who were being interviewed on their golden wedding anniversary. "In all that time—did you ever consider divorce?" they were asked.

"Oh, no, not divorce," the little old lady said, "but sometimes,"—she paused and winked at her husband—"murder!"

Every marriage has problems. They are inevitable.

Two newlyweds are like two planets that have been going around the sun at different speeds in different orbits. Now they are in the same orbit. Unless they adjust their rate of travel they will crash.[1] Adjust they must. But such adjustments are neither easy nor instantaneous.

The difference between a good marriage and a bad marriage is that the former couple has learned to solve problems. Without this ability a good marriage is impossible. With this ability frustration is changed to fulfillment. Skill in solving problems is of such critical importance no two persons are prepared for marriage until they have mastered it.

But how? How are problems solved?

Jay Adams has helpfully shown there are four basic approaches to any problem.[2]

1. *Go Around It*

"It does not matter; it's unimportant; I'll just simply avoid it."

2. *Go Aside From It*

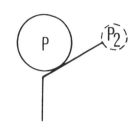

"It isn't what I wanted anyway; this isn't the course I wanted to take." He allows the problem to deflect him from his course and often manufactures a false problem as a camouflage.

3. *Go Back From It*

"It simply can't be done; it's impossible; it's hopeless; I give up."

4. *Go Through It*

"It can be solved through Christ."

It is only in the fourth approach that the problem is solved. Boldly and confidently the couple says "This problem can be solved by the power of the Spirit of God and the application of the Word of God."

In this chapter we will examine eight problem-solving principles and relate them to your marriage. More than this, you will be given an opportunity to explore the Scriptures for yourselves and to formulate other principles that are particularly relevant to your relationship.

Now for some time-tested texts that may make all the difference in your married life.

First, Be Truthful

Therefore, laying aside falsehood, speak truth, each one of you, with his neighbor, for we are members of one another (Eph. 4:25).

(1) *Truthful speaking involves speaking.*

The silent treatment may avoid controversy; it may frustrate and punish your spouse; it may protect you from hurt; but it will never resolve a conflict. "Silence is golden" as the saying goes. Someone has said it also can be yellow! Don't hide behind silence because you are afraid to deal with a problem.

Marriage counselors estimate that at least one half of the cases they see involve a silent husband. How do you encourage a silent person to talk?

Determine why he has become silent and deal with the root problem.[3]

Allow him to choose the time to speak (don't pressure him to talk to you).

When he speaks listen without judging what he says. Accept his feelings and frustrations. Make it a positive experience.[4]

(2) *Truthful speaking says it straight.*

It is not devious but direct. It is not a flood of broad generalities but it is a stream of concrete specifics. It is saying what I really mean! "The aim of argument, or of discussion, should not be victory, but progress" according to Joseph Joubert.[5] Most of us would agree. Without straight talking, there can be little progress.

(3) *Truthful speaking avoids exaggerations.*

The easiest thing in the world is to exaggerate. Carefully avoid words like "never," "always," "all," or "everyone." Sweeping generalizations are seldom the truth.

(4) *Truthful speaking admits a wrong.*

According to Samuel Butler: "From a worldly point of view, there is no mistake so great as that of always being right." The man who will not admit he has been wrong loves himself more than he loves the truth. "The man who refuses to admit his mistakes can never be successful" (Prov. 28:13, LB). "An apology is a good way to have the last word!"

SECOND, BE QUICK TO RECONCILE

Be angry, and yet do not sin; do not let the sun go down on your anger, and do not give the devil an opportunity (Eph. 4:26–27).

This word is custom made from the husband-wife scene. After all, where is one more liable to get angry than living in the same house, with the same person week after week? The average marriage is crowded with situations and circumstances that breed anger.

Anger may be a strong emotion of displeasure, it may be a reaction to some sinful conduct, or it may be righteous indignation. On the other hand, it may be the result of frustration or the response to not getting your own way. "If you are angry, don't sin" (LB). But how can we avoid it? How should we handle anger?

Norman Wright points out there are at least four basic reactions to anger.[6]

(1) We suppress it—when we recognize we are angry and try to keep it under control. According to Proverbs 29:11, this is the mark of a wise man. There is, however, a problem here. If we constantly suppress our anger we will eventually build up such a head of steam there will be a massive eruption.

(2) We express it—when we let it all hang out. Generally we feel better after we have yelled or screamed. Often we get results too, but usually the results are counterproductive!

(3) We repress it—when we deny the existence of our anger. This is surely the worst possible response. It is a hazard to our health and our home.

(4) We confess it—when we get it out in the open, assuming responsibility for our own emotions and determining to work out the problem.

Paul leaves us in no doubt concerning the urgency of the situation. Delays in reconciliation are not only blatantly sinful, they are also mighty dangerous. "When you are angry you give a mighty foothold for the devil" (LB).

Often I am asked who should take the first step. The answer: You, whoever you are, always!

"But," you say, "it is his (or her) fault. He (or she) is the one who has wronged me." Matthew 18:15 instructs you to take the first step to effect a reconciliation.

If you have wronged your spouse or even if your spouse feels you are at fault, our Lord directs you again to initiate the reconciliation (Matt. 5:23).

You see, the issue is not who is at fault. Irrespective of this, *you* are to go.

Here is a helpful hint. Enter into a covenant with your partner never to go to sleep without kissing her good night. It is a very difficult thing to kiss your wife if you are angry! More times than you can imagine, this will precipitate a reconciliation and solve a problem. It is not too early to implement this principle now. Commit yourselves to it as to a word from God. Never separate from each other angry. Resolve the issue first. Not only will you gain a good night's sleep but you will also develop a pattern that will make your marriage something special.

According to Confucius, "Men do not stumble over mountains, but over molehills." The breakdown of most marriages can be traced to the build-up of small, insignificant but unresolved problems. Learn to deal with your anger biblically. It may save your life.

THIRD, BE HONEST AND GENEROUS

Let him who steals steal no longer; but rather let him labor, performing with his own hands what is good, in order that he may have something to share with him who has need (Eph. 4:28).

Thieves come in all shapes and sizes.

Husbands may be surprised to find out that they may take from their wives individuality and identity. They may demand services and sacrifices to which they have no right. They daily rob their wives of the love, honor, and leadership they owe to them. Such husbands are no better than thankless thieves.

Wives, too, can steal from their husbands. You have met women who rob their husbands of self-respect and self-confidence. They usurp the position and authority of their mate. They demand pity and consideration, things to which they have no right. They rob their husbands of the respect, love, submission, and help they owe to them.

When such selfishness is replaced with generous giving, problems will be resolved. Remember: at the very core of love is the spirit of giving. It was our Lord, Himself, who said, "It is more blessed to give than to receive" (Acts 20:35).

Approach a problem with this attitude and you will be amazed at its speedy elimination.

FOURTH, BE POSITIVE AND CONSTRUCTIVE

Let no unwholesome word proceed from your mouth, but only such a word as is good for edification according to the need of the moment, that it may give grace to those who hear. And do not grieve the Holy Spirit of God, by whom you were sealed for the day of redemption (Eph. 4:29–30).

Unwholesome words are spiteful, harmful, hurtful, hateful words. They cut a person down or tear a person up. Invariably you will find such words in the midst of a marriage problem. Often they cause it. Sometimes they aggravate it. Occasionally they terminate it—permanently! Approaching a problem with these kinds of words is like coming to a fire with a gallon of gasoline. You can expect an explosion.

It is of great significance to observe the intimate relationship between verses 29 and 30. The latter begins with "and," a conjunction that ties the warning of this verse to the injunction of the previous verse. What is Paul saying? Simply this: It is the misuse of your tongue that grieves the Holy Spirit! What a solemn note. Unhealthy, unwholesome, and unhelpful words not only malign mates; they also grieve the Spirit of God.

More times than you can imagine, the solution to a domestic disruption is either the right use of words or in the use of right words. Such words, according to Paul, possess three qualities.

Frustration or Fulfillment

(1) *They are positive, not negative*—"good for edification." They encourage, build up, and strengthen the hearer.

(2) *They are directed at the problem, not the person*— "according to the need of the moment." They are addressed to the problem at hand, not the person at fault. It is never difficult to determine where one's words are directed. Before you speak, pause. Reflect on the first word in the flood of verbiage that is about to pour forth. When the sentence begins "You . . . ," the words are directed at the person not the problem—and they should never escape from your lips. Speak only words that are apt and appropriate, words that are timely. Such words will help and heal.

(3) *They build, not destroy*—"that it may give grace to those who hear." Here is the elimination of the irritation. "Good" words break through problems, resolve deadlocks, and rebuild broken bridges.

Let all bitterness and wrath and anger and clamor and slander be put away from you, along with all malice. And be kind to one another, tender-hearted, forgiving each other, just as God in Christ also has forgiven you (Eph. 4:31–32).

Many a marriage problem traced to its source will bring you to verse 31. Somewhere you will discover one of these six hideous monsters. What a contaminating cesspool is the human heart. It is out of this corruption that problems both emerge and grow. It is the manure that feeds the weeds that destroy marriages.

The remedy offered in verse 32 has been proven a thousand times over—be kind, tender-hearted, forgiving.[7]

A. Why?
1. Because if you don't forgive you will begin to retaliate and seek revenge. Revenge is God's business (Rom. 12:19).
2. Because God will forgive you the way you forgive others (Matt. 6:12–15).
3. Because your offenses against God are far greater than anything your spouse could do against you— and God has forgiven you (Matt. 18:21–35).

4. Because if you don't forgive, you will become emotionally enslaved to your offending spouse. (See story of Esau's enslavement to Jacob, Gen. 33.)

B. How?

"Just as God in Christ also has forgiven you." That means freely, fully, irreversibly! When you find this difficult:

Remember how God has forgiven you—and your debt to God was far greater.

Realize how God has used your partner and the problem to mold your life, and thank God for this.

Recognize your responsibility in the problem and confess what you have contributed toward the problem.

Resolve to pray for your spouse assisting and helping in any way possible.

Be forgiving—no home can survive without it.

Sixth, Be Christlike

The very unity and life of the church at Philippi was threatened by the problem of internal dissension. Although we do not know the cause of the strife we are left in no doubt as to its solution.

In Philippians 2:3–4 Paul exhorts his readers to cultivate the attitude of Christ toward each other. What does this involve?

Be selfless—"do nothing from selfishness."

Be sacrificial—"regard one another as more important than himself."

Be serving—"look out . . . for the interests of others."

Lest there be any misunderstanding, Paul presents to us a real-life example of the recommended mind set. The pattern, of course, is our Lord Himself. To look at Him in Philippians 2:5–8 is to understand precisely Paul's words in verses 3–4. Our Lord, in His humiliation, was selfless, sacrificial, and serving. Here is the model for every believer in a situation of strife and conflict. This is the mind set we are to cultivate and demonstrate.

Because this was His attitude in dealing with my sin I am to demonstrate this same attitude in dealing with problems between my wife and me. It will work every time. But what a price to pay! If verses 5–8 are not sufficient motivation for you, try verses 9–11. "Therefore also God highly exalted Him. . . ." What an encouragement! The One who humbled Himself, God exalted. Do you see the point?

This three-dimensional attitude is the biblical answer to scores of problems that have disrupted and destroyed marriages for centuries. Learn the principle well. Store it up in your memory bank—but keep it handy. You will need it often.

SEVENTH, BE GRACIOUS

Do not judge lest you be judged yourselves. For in the way you judge, you will be judged; and by your standard of measure, it shall be measured to you. And why do you look at the speck in your brother's eye, but do not notice the log that is in your own eye?

Or how can you say to your brother, "Let me take the speck out of your eye," and behold, the log is in your own eye? You hypocrite, first take the log out of your own eye, and then you will see clearly enough to take the speck out of your brother's eye (Matt. 7:1–5).

Any marriage counselor is able to draw from his files a score of cases involving irate wives who have poured out a pile of faults big enough to bury their husbands, or of frustrated husbands who have fired off a deadly barrage of accusations against their wives. Such situations seem to defy solution. Yet it is to that very situation that our Lord speaks in our text. He begins with a prohibition: "Do not judge." On the surface this is just a little remarkable, because in verse 6 He tells us to judge. Surely Christians are to use their discretion. We must show discernment and discrimination. What then does our Lord mean in this verse? Because the verb used here is capable of a wide variety of meanings, it must be understood in the light of the context. In Matthew 7 the judging that is in view, I believe, is that of condemning an individual. It involves giving a final verdict, passing sentence upon someone, making a condemning judgment.

According to our Lord, we ought not pass final verdicts for three reasons:

(1) "Lest you be judged yourself." Those who put themselves in the position of being judges of others will some day be judged by the Lord at the judgment seat of Christ. There they will give an account of the judgment they have made of another. For this reason we ought not to condemn others.

(2) You set a standard for your own judgment. The Lord says, "For in the way you judge, you will be judged; and by your standard of measure, it shall be measured to you." By judging others, you set your own standard for judgment. The man who takes upon himself the authority of making a final judgment about his wife is going to be judged by Christ as one who has assumed for himself the final authority in judgment. He will be held more responsible. He will receive more severe consequences. The wife who is very sharp, quick, and dogmatic in making final judgments about her husband's behavior or attitude will be judged as someone who was scrupulous and meticulous in judgment. She will be held much more responsible. She will receive more severe judgment. For this reason a Christian ought never make a final judgment. We ought never condemn another individual.

(3) "Because you are not capable of judging" (vv. 3–5). That is of the greatest importance. Why are you incapable of making a judgment? It is because you have a log in your eye. What is this log? How is it to be interpreted? The Lord says that you have something in your life that is bigger, that is greater, that is more harmful and more destructive than the speck you have noticed in the eye of your wife. What is that? I am inclined to believe, within the context of the passage, that it is the spirit of criticism. He is saying that the passion to criticize is bigger and greater than the sin that is in the life of the person you are criticizing. Your wife may be guilty of any one of a number of failures, but if you have a spirit of criticism against her, you have something in your life that, by God's standards, is bigger and more serious than the fault or failure in your wife's life. It makes you incapable of making an accurate judgment.

More than that, you are also incapable of helping your partner with her speck of a problem. The Lord says, "Or how can you say to your brother, 'Let me take the speck out of your eye, and behold, the log is in your own eye?'" (v. 4). How would you like to have an opthamologist working on a little piece of steel in the corner of your eye when he had in his eye a big piece of steel? You see, removing specks from eyes is a difficult task. It demands professional skill. It requires calmness, coolness, patience, and control. To help your partner, compassion, tenderness, and sensitivity are required. It involves tears and weeping. The man or woman who has a spirit of criticism is incapable of helping. That is not all. The Lord goes on to say you are not only incapable of judging and incapable of helping, but you are insincere about helping. I conclude that from the first phrase in verse 5. He says to the critic, "You hypocrite." The person, then, with a critical spirit, who comes to his wife pointing out to her a fault, or two faults, is not really sincere about helping her. He may say, "Now, honey, I am just trying to be helpful," but if he has the spirit of criticism in his life, he is not being helpful. He is a hypocrite. He is bringing things to the surface in order to either deflate his wife or elevate himself.

What is the proper course of action? "First take the log out of your own eye, and then you will see clearly enough to take the speck out of your brother's eye." If our Lord is teaching anything here, He is surely exhorting us to eliminate the spirit of criticism. This is a "must." Judge that spirit of criticism before the Lord. Ask for forgiveness and freedom. When that spirit of criticism is gone you will be able to see clearly enough to help her take the speck out of her life. Only then will you be in a position to help. Only then will you be in a position to encourage the development of that quality of character that is so essential in your marriage relationship. But you will never be able to help until first of all you have taken the log out of your own eye!

EIGHTH, BE PATIENT AND PRAYERFUL

For you have been called for this purpose, since Christ also suffered for you, leaving you an example for you to follow in His steps, Who committed no sin, nor was any deceit found in His mouth; and while being reviled, He did not revile in return; while suffering, He uttered no threats, but kept entrusting Himself to Him who judges righteously (1 Peter 2:21–23).

Here is surely one of the most difficult principles in all the Word of God to implement in our lives. Our Lord again is the pattern to follow. He has left us a model of righteous suffering and has given it that we might follow in His steps. Notice carefully the pathway He has set out for every believer—for every marriage partner:

Step 1: clean conduct before suffering (v. 22).
Step 2: calm conduct during suffering (v. 23a).
Step 3: complete commitment during suffering (v. 23b).

These three steps will preserve your marriage from one of its most devastating enemies. Occasionally you will be misunderstood by your partner. You may even be treated unfairly, accused unjustly. How will you respond? In some cases, where communication is impossible, follow the pattern of our Lord! If you are innocent, be calm and quiet. Commit your case to God. As in His time He vindicated His Son, so in His time He will vindicate you.

There they are, eight principles for solving problems. They are hardly original and certainly not new to most of us. Actually, they are quite obvious, aren't they? The trick is to know how to use them.

A friend of mine has an instrument he uses to test his electrical system and diagnose problems under the hood of his car. I know all about that instrument, but I have never learned to use it. I have often admired him as I have watched him work with it. I know what it is designed to do, but I am unable to achieve anything with it.

That is the way many of us are with these principles. From our earliest days we may have known them, but have we learned when and how to use each one? We are not really ready for married life until we have developed the ability to handle each one skillfully, until they are part of our life style.

Beware! "The spirit indeed is willing, but the flesh is weak." Do not rely on the flesh in the midst of spiritual combat. The flesh is so weak, and it is only by the enablement of the Holy Spirit in a Spirit-controlled life that these obvious principles become operative.

If you expect perfection from your spouse, your life will be a series of disappointments, grumblings, and complaints. If, however, you have realistic expectations, taking your spouse as a human creature which he/she is, you will undoubtedly be surprised.

There will be problems. There always are. Yet God will use them to mature and perfect both you and your relationship as you confront them biblically.

Notes

[1]Donald Grey Barnhouse, *God's Covenants, God's Discipline, God's Glory*, Rom. 9:1–16:27 (Grand Rapids: Eerdmans, 1973), p. 23.

[2]Jay E. Adams, *Competent to Counsel* (Nutley, New Jersey: Presbyterian and Reformed Publishing Company, 1970), pp. 129–130.

[3]See: H. Norman Wright, *Communication: Key to Your Marriage* (Glendale, California: Regal Books, 1974), p. 66.

[4]Ibid., p. 140.

[5]Quoted by Dan Benson, *The Total Man* (Wheaton: Tyndale, 1977), p. 165.

[6]H. Norman Wright, *Communication: Key to Your Marriage*, pp. 87–93.

[7]I am indebted to Bill Gothard, Institute of Basic Youth Conflicts, for some of the principles discussed here.

Project Page

1. You now have eight biblical principles that will be invaluable in solving problems in your married years. Can you list all eight of them, supporting each one with its Scripture text?

2. Which of these principles are you already using to resolve your problems?

3. Which principle do you find the most difficult to implement? Why? What steps do you propose to take toward mastering it?

4. What other principles would you like to add to the list? These principles should be ones you have been using in your relationship to ones you sense an urgent need to implement.

19 Pondering Through Proverbs

Someone has well called the Book of Proverbs "A Guidebook for Successful Living." It is just that.

Picture, if you will, a wise and experienced father taking his teen-age son aside, and sitting him down for an intimate heart-to-heart talk on the hard facts of life. The content of that chat is preserved for us in Proverbs. An investment of time in this book now will yield rich dividends in your married life to come.

A PROJECT FOR BOTH OF YOU

The Book of Proverbs contains thirty-one chapters—one for each day of the month. Let me strongly urge you to read this book together over the next month. Take one chapter a day. Whenever possible, read it together. When you cannot be together, read the chapter for that day independently.

A PROJECT FOR THE FIANCÉ

The most efficient and practical way of studying the Book of Proverbs is to attack it topically. Almost every conceivable subject is addressed by the authors in this remarkable book. For the profit of your marriage, we have chosen four topics for you to examine in some detail.[1]

Under each of the following subjects, study the suggested texts carefully. Write out, in your own words, the lesson of the verse. At the conclusion of each topical study write down two or three applications of the study you plan to make in your marriage. When you have completed the chapter share with your fiancée the decisions you have made as a result of your study. (Caution: Some of those decisions may need to be revised to include your fiancée's point of view!)

1. *Speech*
   a. A wise man knows the influence of his words. What are they able to do?

   18:21—explain this verse.

   12:18

   16:27–28

   16:24

   Because your words have the power to _____ you (13:3), or the power to _____ you (12:14), you ought to be cautious before you speak and use only _____ words.

b. A wise man knows the limitations of his words. He
understands they are no substitute for
(14:23). Words cannot alter the   (28:24).
Because words alone can never compel a response
(29:19), what must a marriage partner have in order to
gain a response to his/her words?

c. Consider the marks of good words according to the
following verses.

12:22   18:8

10:19   11:13

26:28   6:12–15

27:2   17:14

19:13   25:11

Life Responses—for your marriage:

1.

2.

3.

2. *Money*
   a. A wise man knows the limitations of money. What are the limitations?

   15:16–17

17:1

23:4–5

30:8–9

b. A wise man knows the value of money. Identify the use of money in each of these verses.

10:22

14:20–21

30:8–9

10:15

c. A wise man knows how to obtain money. How?

10:3

15:6

10:4

11:24–26

20:21

24:27

d. A wise man knows how to use his money. What principles for budgeting are prescribed in these verses?

3:9–10

3:27–28

19:17

Read also: 1 Corinthians 16:2; 2 Corinthians 9:6-7; 1 Timothy 6:5-19; Hebrews 13:5.

Life Responses—for your marriage:

1.

2.

3.

3. *Christian character*
   Explain the quality of Christian character presented in each of the following proverbs and apply it to a marriage relationship.

   a. 1:7

b. 3:5–6

c. 28:13

d. 16:6

e. 10:8

f. 13:5

g. 17:27

h. 14:29

i. 19:11

j. 10:12

k. 13:16

l. 14:15–16

4. *The family*

   Remember, Proverbs is addressed to the king's son. It is therefore primarily instructive for the husband.

   a. The wise man's relationship to his wife.

      According to 18:22; 19:14 he

      According to 12:4 he

      According to 5:18, 21; 6:24–29 he

   b. The wise man's relationship to his children. According to the following proverbs what will be your responsibility to your children?

      23:13–14

1:8

22:6

Life Responses—for your marriage.

1.

2.

3.

A wise man, according to Proverbs, is a person who lives his life well. His life is orderly, productive, and attractive. He is skilled in living life and his skill is evident in his use of the tongue, his attitude toward money, his character in general, and his role in the family.

This is precisely the wisdom James had in mind when he wrote:

> But the wisdom from above is first pure, then peaceable, gentle, reasonable, full of mercy and good fruits, unwavering, without hypocrisy. And the seed whose fruit is righteousness is sown in peace by those who make peace (James 3:17–18).

How is such skill to be gained? For many it comes through experience. Solomon might well ask, "Why learn the hard way? Learn from my experience!" Someone has said:

The philosophy of the world is "Live and learn."
The philosophy of Proverbs is "Learn and live."

It is only a fool who does not learn from the experience of others. Although experience is a good teacher, she also is a hard teacher.

For the Christian there is an alternative. Direction and instruction in living our lives well is freely available to us in books such as Proverbs. Having learned how to live our lives we are encouraged to turn to the Lord for the enabling grace.

> But if any of you lacks wisdom, let him ask of God, who gives to all men generously and without reproach, and it will be given to him (James 1:5).

Here is the answer to our plaintive cry, "How?" This moral skill is generously bestowed by God on all His children who sincerely wait on Him.

Once again, the quality of your married life will be the most accurate thermometer measuring the warmth or coldness of your spiritual life. It will be the telltale sign to all. The cultivation of your personal walk with the Lord is the best preparation you can ever make for your marriage. How is it going?

Notes

[1]My indebtedness is acknowledged to Dr. Bruce Waltke of Regent College, Vancouver, B.C., whose work on Proverbs has been a great personal blessing and is reflected in the projects of this and the following chapter.

20 An Excellent Wife

He who finds a wife finds a good thing, And obtains favor from the LORD (Prov. 18:22).

This is especially true if she is an excellent wife. Fortunately, we are left in no doubt as to the character of such a person. Her portrait is sketched for us in Proverbs 31:10–31.

Perhaps the most helpful way to isolate her qualities is to explore her various relationships as they appear in these verses. This will not only give you a tidy handle on the passage but also a beautiful model to emulate.

PROJECT FOR THE FIANCÉE

Beware: this could be a life-changing experience. If you have already read Jay Adams on this topic you know what I mean.[1] Now you are ready to do some digging on your own. As you analyze the various aspects of each relationship quietly pray that the Lord will grant you the grace to be this kind of wife.

Perhaps a simple overview of the passage will be useful. Read the verses using the following outline:

   I. The Introduction (v. 10). An excellent wife is described as a rare and valuable creature.
   II. The Description (vv. 11–27). She is described in terms of several relationships.
   III. The Conclusion (vv. 28–31). She is praised by her children, husband, and friends.

The object of this project is to isolate the character qualities of an excellent wife in the various relationships of her life. Study carefully verses 11–27. Then record all you can discover about this wife under the appropriate relationship.

A. *She is a good mother.*
   Focus here on her relationship to her children. How would you describe her?

   verses 14–15

   verses 21–22

   verse 27

B. *She is a good wife.*
   Describe her relationship to her husband as portrayed in these verses.

   verse 11a

verses 11b–12

verse 22

verse 23

C. *She is a good homemaker.*
Consider her relationship to her home. The scope of her influence and activity is vast indeed.

> It shows the full flowering of domesticity which is revealed as no petty and restricted sphere.[2]

What do the following verses indicate about her interests and involvements?

verses 13–14

verse 16

Note, however, that all her gifts and abilities are being used for her home! They contribute to the house rather than distract from it. Her home is her priority.

D. *Her relationship to her neighbors.*
   What kind of a neighbor is she?

   verses 20, 26

   verse 26

E. *She is a good woman.*
   From the verses below isolate four qualities of character that qualify her as a good woman.

   verse 13

   verses 15, 17, 19, 27

verses 13, 16, 18

verse 25

This is one of the most beautiful descriptions of personhood to be found in all literature.

She seems to be the personification of all the virtues and strengths of character urged upon us throughout Proverbs. She is a model for us all, whether men, women or children.[3]

Proverbs 31:10–31 presents the Bible's most complete and beautiful picture of what a good wife should be. She is capable, ambitious, a willing worker; she is kind, wise, trustworthy, cheerful, providing for her household and reaching beyond. She knows her worth. She uses, to good purpose, her intelligence, her physical strength, her God-fearing character. She makes life abundant for her husband, their children, and for the poor and needy beyond their family circle. A remarkable woman![4]

The emphasis in this choice piece of Hebrew poetry is on character. What could be of greater importance in choosing a mate? Begin to ask the Lord to mold you into this kind of person. Before you pray, consider this:

What is the secret of her success? You will find it in verse 30.

Explain what this means.

In this magnificent piece of Hebrew poetry, King Lemuel records for us the instructions he has received from his mother regarding the choice of a wife. What kind of a woman is fit for a king? The kind described here. What kind of a woman should he seek for his wife? A woman of this character! The emphasis, throughout, is on character. What could be of greater importance in choosing a partner?

Begin to ask the Lord, now, to mold you into this type of woman and wife. Keeping the qualities of Proverbs 31:10–31 in mind, write below your prayer to God.

Notes

[1]Jay Adams, *Christian Living In the Home* (Nutley, New Jersey; Presbyterian and Reformed Publishing Company, 1972), pp. 77–84.

[2]Derek Kidner, *The Proverbs* (Downers Grove, Ill: InterVarsity Press, 1964), p. 184.

[3]James T. Draper Jr., *Proverbs* (Wheaton: Tyndale, 1971), p. 147.

[4]Larry Christenson, *The Christian Family* (Minneapolis: Bethany Fellowship, 1970), p. 34.

21   Keys to a Happy Home

I have yet to meet a couple who did not want a happy home. You're not surprised, of course. I'm sure you have found the same to be true. Nor have I ever met an engaged couple who did not expect to have a happy marriage. After all, they would be most foolish to enter into matrimony if this was not their expectation. You wouldn't, would you? You want a happy home. You expect a happy marriage. But what are your chances?

Dr. Ed Wheat, in his excellent set of cassettes on "Sex Techniques and Sex Problems in Marriage," states that sociologists have conclusively demonstrated the five major factors contributing to happy marriages.[1]

Using the chart below, do a personal evaluation of your relationship in respect to each of these five factors. Think carefully and critically. Be open and honest.

MAJOR FACTORS   PERSONAL EVALUATION

1. Seeing a happy marriage in your home as you grew up.

2. Adequate time in courtship and engagement.

3. Adequate sexual information.

4. Financial stability.

5. Emotional maturity.

172

In earlier chapters we discussed the second and fifth of these factors. The remaining three each warrant a brief comment.

Some of you, perhaps many of you, have been deprived of the privilege of seeing a happy marriage in your home. Your parents had problems. You were exposed to a poor example. Your model was not the best. Perhaps it was the worst it could possibly be. You have almost unconsciously assimilated attitudes and values from your upbringing that could bring down your marriage.

It is, of course, too late to turn the clock back. This is now history. The damage has been done. Fortunately, it is not irrevocable. To realize that your childhood experiences now pose a threat to the happiness of your marriage is to be on guard against the enemy and to take steps toward a counterattack. If you have been conditioned by a poor pattern you need to be deprogrammed. The most effective "deprogrammer" is the Holy Spirit, who uses the Word of God to reprove, correct, and instruct (2 Tim. 3:16). Hopefully, this is exactly what has been happening as you have been studying this course together. The way out and back is neither easy nor short, but God is sufficient. Prayerfully wait on Him to transform your attitudes through the renewing ministry of the Spirit. Diligently immerse yourself in the principles and precepts of Holy Scripture. They are a lamp for your feet—a light for your path (Ps. 119:105).

At this point, some of you may feel slightly deficient in adequate sexual knowledge. This is no problem. We have still to deal with this subject in our program. Next month you will be asked to read *The Act of Marriage* by Tim LaHaye, a book that will supply you with all the information you will need—and more. Also both of you will be asked to have a thorough physical examination by your family physician. This will afford you a splendid opportunity to pursue any questions on this subject that still linger in your mind.

Financial stability is a major consideration for any marriage in our topsy-turvy world. Some counselors maintain that the problem of finances is the number one problem in marriages today. There is some excellent material available on this subject for any young couple seeking assistance. Let me recommend two sources you may find helpful:

1. Dan Benson, *The Total Man* (Wheaton: Tyndale, 1977). Chapter 16—"Until Debt Do Us Part." Chapter 17—"Five Safeguards of Your Financial Freedom."
2. Larry Burkett, "Christian Financial Concepts." A Cassette Bible Study Course in: God's Principles of Handling Money. Bible Believers Cassettes, Inc., 130 N. Spring St., Springdale, Ark. 72764.

Here they are: five keys to a happy home. Before your marriage you need to examine them carefully. When these five areas are in order you are ready for Part Four: Your Wedding and After!

Notes

[1]This set of tapes may be obtained through Bible Believers Cassettes, Inc., 130 N. Spring St., Springdale, Arkansas, 72764.

Projects for Next Month

1. Complete Part Four of your study guide.

2. Read: LaHaye, *The Act of Marriage*.

3. Be prepared to discuss the biblical purposes of a sexual relationship and the implications of 1 Corinthians 7:1–5 to your marriage.

4. During this month both of you ought to have thorough physical examinations by your family physician. You will want to discuss with him the subject of contraception.

Part Four

Your Wedding
and After

22 Setting Your Goals

He who has a program without a vision is a worker
He who has a vision without a program is a dreamer
He who has a vision and a program is a conqueror.
—*H. Hendricks*

This chapter is designed to assist you in sharpening the focus on your marriage goals. Without goals you will be going nowhere in particular. With goals, every step in your married life takes on tremendous significance. Thoughtfully work together through the following projects.

1. What are the biblical goals of marriage? Study carefully the following passages: Genesis 2:18–24; Ephesians 5:22–23; Malachi 2:14; Deuteronomy 6:4–8, plus others you feel important. In view of all you have studied, formulate a list of biblical goals for your marriage. Record them on the chart on the following page.

2. A functional goal is simply a step to be taken toward achieving a biblical goal. For example:

    Biblical goal: to know Christ intimately (Phil. 3:10).
    Functional goal: a daily quiet time for prayer and reading the Scriptures.
    a daily period of meditation on the glories of Christ.
    to read one book each month on the person and work of Christ.

    What functional goals are you prepared to set for each of your biblical goals? These are the immediate steps you will take to achieve that long-term goal.

Record your functional goals on the following chart.

BIBLICAL GOALS	FUNCTIONAL GOALS
1.	1.
	2.
	3.
2.	1.
	2.
	3.
3.	1.
	2.
	3.
4.	1.
	2.
	3.

OPTIONAL PROJECT

(For the very hearty, only)

Each of you write a personal private letter to the other. In this letter, express in as much detail as possible, with clear illustrations and Scriptures, what you wish your marriage partner to be.

Suggestion: Use the third person. For example:
"I wish her (my wife) to be. . . ."
"I am asking God for a wife who will. . . ."

Exchange your letters. Accept your letter as a personal goal to be achieved for the glory of God and the joy and blessing of your spouse. Read it carefully. Pray over it constantly. Ask the Lord to enable you to be this kind of partner for the one you love.

Keep the letters in a safe place. They will make interesting reading in front of the fireplace on the evening of your wedding anniversary!

23   "One Flesh," and . . .

One of the most significant of all biblical passages on the sexual relationship of a husband and wife is 1 Corinthians 7:1–7. Perhaps a contemporary paraphrase will make it even more meaningful.

> If . . . you want to refrain from sexual relations for a time, by all means feel free to do so. But be careful not to let such conjugal vacations last too long. You are, after all, only human, with understandable human appetites and needs. And if you deny those over an extended period, you weaken your resistance to temptation. Remember that the city of Corinth in particular abounds in temptation, in constant opportunities and inducements to satisfy sexual desires. Therefore, you wives, if your husbands are obviously in need of sexual expression, do not deny them. And you husbands, show a like consideration for your wives. You are both far better off to give your sexual needs satisfaction in your marital relationship than to be guilty of adultery with another, either in action or inner thought and desire. And if you are aflame with passion, it is clear that you cannot please the Lord. So if your libidinal urges are strong, you had better maintain a vigorous sex life within your marriage. In doing this you do not sin.[1]

1. What are the implications of this passage for:

   a. you as a husband?

b. you as a wife?

2. Often I am asked a question that goes something like this: "What is acceptable and proper between a husband and wife in the privacy of their bedroom?" Such questions can only be answered by principles. Considering such elements as selfless love, mutual esteem, and common consent, form three principles that will serve you as helpful guidelines.

   a.

   b.

   c.

Without God, the regulation of the sex life in marriage is either a compromise in which each partner hides his real thoughts from the other, or else tyranny of one over the other, or it may be an artificial and rigid edifice of formal principles. No moral or psychological system can regulate by principles a domain which belongs to daily obedience to God, to the free submission to Him of the conscience enlightened by the Scriptures and the teachings of the Church. When God directs the sex life of a couple, they can practice it divinely, if I may use the word—in a full, mutual communion that is carnal, moral, and spiritual all at once. It is the crowning symbol of their total giving of themselves to each other.[2]

3. For further study and exposure on this subject I highly recommend:

Intended For Pleasure by Ed Wheat M.D. and Gaye Wheat (Fleming H. Revell Company, 1977). An excellent book on sex technique and sexual fulfillment in Christian marriage. Illustrated.

Also,

Sexual Technique and Sex Problems in Marriage by Ed Wheat M.D.

Bible Believers Cassettes Inc.,
130 N. Spring,
Springdale, Ark. 72764.

Notes

[1]Wm. Cole, *Sex and Love In The Bible* (New York: Associated Press, 1959), pp. 293–294.
[2]Paul Tournier, *The Healing of Persons* (New York: Harper and Row, 1964), p. 179.

24   Family Planning

Children are love made visible.   —*Robert C. Dodds*

Children are a gift of the Lord.   —*Psalm 127:3*

During the visit with your doctor you may wish to discuss the subject of birth control. Reading *The Act of Marriage* (LaHaye) will be a helpful preparation for this discussion. Before consultation with your doctor you will need to decide together about the question of contraception in your marriage.

PROJECTS

1. Read carefully the following quotation from Helmut Thielicke.

   The fetus has its own autonomous life, which despite all of its reciprocal relationship to the maternal organism is more than a mere part of this organism and possesses a certain independence. . . . These elementary biological facts should be sufficient to establish its status as a human being. . . . This makes it clear that here it is not a question—as it is in the case of contraception—whether a proffered gift can be responsibly accepted, but rather whether an already bestowed gift can be spurned, whether one dares to brush aside the arm of God after this arm has already been outstretched. Therefore here (in abortion) the order of creation is infringed upon in a way that is completely different from that of the case of contraception.[1]

2. What is the difference between birth control and abortion?

3. For a more complete discussion of the theological and biblical basis for the practice of contraception consult *Birth Control and the Christian,* ed. Walter O. Spitzer and Carlyle L. Saylor (Wheaton: Tyndale, 1969).

4. What would be some biblical and unbiblical motives for practicing birth control?

Biblical	*Unbiblical*
a) _____	a) _____
b) _____	b) _____
c) _____	c) _____

5. Are you agreed on the principle of birth control? _____

6. If so, have you agreed on the method you will use?_____

Notes

[1]Helmut Thielicke, *The Ethics of Sex* (New York: Harper and Row, 1964), pp. 227–228.

25　The Three Stages of Marriage

The course of many marriages can be easily diagrammed. There are often three stages.

The honeymoon may last one day, one week, one month, or one year, but it will not last forever.

Too often, disillusionment eventually comes. The illusions of an overly idealistic partner are shattered. You begin to question whether you've done the right thing: "Have I made a mistake?" "Maybe we should never have married." While this stage may last for a few minutes or a few days, it will certainly not last forever.

Fulfillment or frustration will inevitably follow, and which one of the two will be determined by how you handle the disillusionment.

In order to ensure a safe passage through these sometimes stormy waters into a tranquil and fulfilling married life, it is necessary to explore more carefully each stage.

A.　The Honeymoon

1. Read Together: Chapter 5, "The Honeymoon," in *Sexual Happiness in Marriage,* Herbert J. Miles (Grand Rapids: Zondervan, 1969).

2. Discuss together the details of your first night. Your fiancee is naturally apprehensive. An open discussion of

what you expect to happen that night will relieve her of any anxieties. Assure her of your care and concern. Agree together on your procedure. Consider her. Let her have a part in the planning. Guarantee her the privacy she may want and the gentleness she will need.

Have you discussed together the details of your first night?_____

3. Plan a spiritual project for your honeymoon. It may be to read a biblical Christian book or even a book of the Bible. It could be to study together a biblical character or subject. Choose a project that will give direction to you for the years ahead—something that will be a real foundation for your marriage.

Here are some suggestions:
Read: *Balancing the Christian Life* (Ryrie)
Hudson Taylor's Spiritual Secret (Taylor)
George Müeller of Bristol (A. T. Pierson)
The Knowledge of the Holy (Tozer)
Study: The Epistle to the Philippians
Principles for Christian Guidance
Memorize: 1 Corinthians 13

What is your spiritual project for your honeymoon?
_____

B. THE DISILLUSIONMENT

1. How may this stage be minimized even to the point that some couples may pass through it without realizing it? Review Part One: "Criteria for Marriage," before you answer!

a.

b.

c.

2. Isolate several key biblical principles that you may apply to your disillusionment. Here are two or three. Add to these several of your own.

   a. 1 Thessalonians 5:18
      It is God's will for me to be thankful in everything.
   b. Ephesians 1:11–12
      God is sovereign. All that happens is within His eternal and wise purpose. This includes our marriage.
   c. Romans 8:28–29.

   d.

   e.

3. How do you plan to cope with disillusionment? What evidences do you have right now that it is the will of God for you to proceed with your marriage? Write them down. Keep them in mind. They will help you cope with any disillusionment if, and when, it comes.

   Fiancé   Fiancée

C. Fulfillment or Frustration

Which will it be in your marriage? Here are two final recommendations. Implement them in your marriage. They virtually guarantee fulfillment!

1. Learn to solve your problems biblically. Every marriage has problems. The difference between frustration and fulfillment often depends upon solving these problems. You have already studied and memorized biblical principles for solving problems. List ten of them below. Support each one with a text. Apply them consistently and prayerfully and God will give the victory.

   a.

   b.

   c.

   d.

e.

f.

g.

h.

i.

j.

2. Introduce the practice of daily devotions. Establish plans now for the family devotions you will begin when you are married. There are four major questions to be considered.

   a. When will you have your devotions?

   _____

   b. Who will lead this time of devotion?

   _____

   c. What will you read and study?

   _____

   d. How will you proceed?

   Here is a suggested format. Try a *P R E P* time.
   — Pray for the Lord's guidance and blessing.
   — Read the selected passage of Scripture together.
   — Examine the verses, applying them to your life.

   Ask: What promise can we claim?
   What warning should we heed?
   What do we learn about Jesus Christ?
   What do we learn about ourselves?
   What example can we follow?
   What do we not understand?

   — Pray together

   Share items for prayer and praise.
   Prayer time together.

It is never too early to introduce this practice into your relationship. It will be an investment of time that will yield dividends of rich blessing in the years ahead. It will bring deep and genuine fulfillment into your marriage.

26 Planning Your Ceremony

If you are Christians you will want your wedding to be a Christian wedding. For myself, there is no experience more beautiful nor more moving than a Christian wedding. It affords a congenial context for presenting the gospel to family, relatives, and friends. For many, it has been an occasion to recall and renew marriage vows that were exchanged years earlier. For you, it will be an opportunity to display publicly the foundations of your new home. It will be a public commitment to a particular life style. It will be a setting of your marriage in a divine direction.

How can you make your ceremony distinctively Christian? This is the aim of our present chapter.

1. Essential Preliminaries

   Rehearsal Date _____ Time _____

               Location _____

   Wedding Date _____ Time _____

             Location _____

   Have these dates and times been reserved? _____

2. Concerning your rehearsal.

   a. Be on time!

   b. Insist on the presence of all members of the bridal party. The parents should be present as well.

c. If you have a professional marriage consultant, invite her also to the rehearsal.

d. Plan at least one hour for the rehearsal.

e. Bring your marriage license to the rehearsal and give it to the person officiating.

f. It will be most helpful at the rehearsal if you have already determined the details of your processional and recessional.

Diagram of your processional.

Diagram of the wedding party at the front of the church.

Diagram of the recessional.

3. Your Vows.

In most situations you will have three options concerning your marriage vows. You may:

a. Leave the choice of vows entirely to the one officiating.

b. Choose from the selection of vows in Appendix B.

c. Write your own vows. If this is the option you choose, the vows ought to be submitted to the person officiating at your last premarriage counseling session. His approval of the vows will undoubtedly be required.

Which of the above three options will you choose?

_____

Do you plan to memorize your vows or to repeat them after the person officiating?

_____

4. A Suggested Order for Your Ceremony

Organ Prelude _____(organist)
Lighting of candles _____(usher)
Seating groom's parents_____(usher or bridegroom)
Seating bride's mother _____(usher or bridegroom)
Enter: officiant, groom, best man.
    As the groom enters, he may wish to greet his mother with a kiss and his father with a warm handshake, expressing his love and appreciation to them.
Processional: Bridesmaids, maid of honor, bride and her father.
    The bride may choose to stop beside her mother and give her a rose, a kiss, or some token of love and appreciation.

Solo: This may be done before the processional or when all the bridal party is present in their positions at the front of the church or chapel.

Title of song _____

Soloist_____

Introduction by the officiant:

—This may be concluded by the father giving away the bride, who may respond by kissing her father before he is seated by his wife.

—Or, you may wish to "Reaffirm Family Ties." See Appendix D.

Message: The officiant may offer a biblical charge to the bride and groom at this point in the ceremony. A message on the "Marks of a Christian Marriage" would be most appropriate.

Invocation

Vows—See the selection of vows in Appendix A
Which selection have you chosen? _____

Exchange of rings. See the selection of vows in Appendix B. Which selection have you chosen?

_____

Pronouncement

Unity candle—See Appendix C.

Salute by groom

Prayer

Solo: Title_____

Benediction

Congratulations by the officiant

Presentation: "It is now my privilege to introduce to you Mr. and Mrs. _____

Recessional

The above order is simply a suggestion. It will offer the options that are before you. Think through your ceremony carefully and be prepared to present a completed order at your final counseling session.

Where the signing of the church register is required by law, I see no reason why this cannot be part of the ceremony itself. On several occasions this has been done on the platform in the front of the congregation. On other occasions it has been done after the ceremony during the time when pictures are being taken.

Your wedding ceremony will be both an ending and beginning. The foundation for your marriage has been laid. Now—the building of your home. May the Lord grant to you both a rich and full life, blessed of God.

But seek first His kingdom and His righteousness; and all these things shall be added to you (Matt. 6:33).

Home is where love lives. Not where it boards, nor pays occasional visits, nor where it may be a sort of permanent guest, with familiar access to certain rooms and cosy corners. But where it owns the front-door key, sits by the glow of a hearthfire of its own kindling, and pervades the whole house with its presence. It may be a king's spacious, luxurious palace. It may be the poor man's narrow-walled cottage, or anywhere in between these two extremes.

There may be present the evidences of wealth and culture and of the sort of refinement that these give, and even the higher refinement they can't give, and yet the place not be a home. And there may be the absence of all this, except the real refinement that love always breeds, and yet, there may be a home, in the sweet, strong meaning of that word.

—*S. D. Gordon*

Appendix A: Marriage Vows

Groom: In God's perfect will and in the presence of these friends, I take you _____ to be my wife, to love, honor, and respect from this day forward, even forever. I promise to provide for you, protect, and defend you as God shall make me able. I will strive without ceasing to edify, encourage, and instruct you according to the command of the Lord Jesus Christ. With the love God has so freely manifested in me I shall endeavor to give likewise this same affection to you. I vow my life to you, trusting in the providence of God, the power of the Holy Spirit, and the authority of the Lord Jesus Christ, in whom *all* things hold together.

Bride: _____, I take you to be my husband and give to you all that I am and have. Through the power and grace of our Lord Jesus Christ I promise to love you with all of my being; to honor, respect, and esteem you above all others, submitting to your loving leadership in all things as unto Christ. I will comfort and care for you, endeavoring always to encourage and edify you. As we are blessed of God with children, I will strive to bring them up in the love of God, instructing them in His ways. As Jesus Christ is the most important person in our lives because He gives us life, I will seek to help you attain the stature and fullness of Christ as we serve Him together, from this day forward and throughout eternity.

Selection 2

If you, then, _____ and _____, have freely and deliberately chosen each other as partners in this holy estate, and know of no just cause why you should not be so united, in token thereof you will please join your right hands.

Groom: _____, in taking the woman you hold by the right hand to be your lawful wedded wife, before God and witnesses present, you must promise to love her, to honor and cherish her in that relationship, and leaving all others cleave only to her, and to be to her in all things a true and faithful husband so long as you both shall live. Do you so promise?

Bride: _____, in taking the man you hold by the right hand to be your lawful wedded husband, before God and the witnesses present, you must promise to love him, honor and cherish him in that relationship, and leaving all others, cleave only to him, and to be to him in all things a true and faithful wife so long as you both shall live. Do you so promise?

Minister's Response:
Then are you each given to the other for richer or poorer, for better or worse, in sickness and in health, till death shall part you.

Selection 3

Officiant: _____, do you take _____, whose hand you hold to be your lawful wedded wife; do you sincerely promise in the presence of this company and in reverence before God, to love, honor, protect her through sunshine and shadow alike, keeping yourself unto her alone until death shall separate you? Do you? (I do.) _____, do you take this man, whose hand you hold, to be your lawful wedded husband; do you sincerely promise in reverence before God and in the presence of this company to be to him a loving, tender, and true wife, through sunshine and shadow alike, keeping yourself unto him alone, until death shall separate you? Do you? (I do.) Now will you repeat these vows.

Groom: I, _____ take thee, _____, to be my wedded wife, to have and to hold from this day forward, for better, for worse, for richer, for poorer, in sickness and in health, to love and to cherish, till death us do part, according to God's holy ordinance, and thereto I pledge thee my love.

And _____, will you likewise repeat these vows.

Bride: I, _____, take thee, _____, to be my wedded husband, to have and to hold from this day forward, for better, for worse, for richer, for poorer, in sickness and in health, to love and to cherish, till death do us part, according to God's holy ordinance, and thereto I pledge thee my love.

Selection 4

Groom: _____, I thank God for you and praise His name that we have both come to know Jesus Christ as our personal Savior. I believe that God has hand-picked you for me and in His perfect will has brought us together to complete each other and be His faithful servants. I need you. I need your love and your total life. As that need is met, I pray that our love for and obedience to Christ will be perfected. That through our relationship, God will demonstrate to the world around us what Jesus Christ can do in an individual life and any relationship. _____, I love you, and before God and these people here, I pledge my life to you. I promise to love you in an understanding way as Christ loves the church. I pledge to care for, to protect, to honor, and to love you no matter what the circumstances might be, until death separates us or Jesus Christ returns to take us home. _____, I believe God has truly brought us together and this love I have for you, no man will put asunder.

Bride: _____, with joy and thanksgiving I accept your pledge of life and love. God said it is not good for man to be alone, so He created me for you to complete you and to be a helpmeet or a helper suitable for you. I need you, _____, and I need your love just as we as Christians need Christ and His love. This life I now commit to you has first been committed to God, and in my commitment to Him, I will commit myself to you; in obedience to Him, I will obey you; in submission to Him, I will submit to you. I give to you now my life and my love and will from this day forward, honor you, respect you, and give to you all that is even yet mine as we are yet two. I will be greatly honored to be your wife, to bear your children, and to grow old with you. I love you, _____, and I can rejoice in knowing that the love I have for you is based on the Word of the living God.

Selection 5

Groom: _____, tonight as I take you to myself to be my life partner, I thank God that in His omniscience He has brought us together. The Word of God teaches that "he who finds a wife has found a good thing, and is blessed by God." I have been blessed by God in finding that good thing in you and I commit my life to the most wonderful gift the Lord has ever given to me; and, _____, know in your heart and in your mind that apart from my own relationship with the Lord, I will cherish nothing more than I do you. I do and will love you as Christ loved the church, His bride, and I will honor you as a child of God and as my divinely chosen wife. All that I have and all that I am, I give to you. And, I will love you until death do us part or until the Lord comes again and takes us both home to be with Him for eternity. I adore you, I need you, and from this day forth I belong to you and to you alone.

Bride: _____, because we are both at peace in the assurance that our Lord planned and blesses our coming together, I entrust my life and my love to you from this day forward.

I come to you with my need for your strength, your understanding, and your tender care—needs you have so lovingly developed in me by completely filling them for me.

I will strive with Christ's help to be a sensitive, gentle, and godly wife, and with His strength and guidance I'll stand with you through everything. I'll laugh with you and share your happiness, but as well, I'll comfort you in your sadness. I'll care for you when you're ill. I'll honor you in your hours of strength. And, I'll joyfully submit to you as the head of our home because I respect you and your integrity and because God planned that it should be this way.

Forsaking all others I will keep myself to you until death shall temporarily separate us. And with our own love molded and directed by our Father in heaven, we will become one even while we are yet two.

Selection 6

Groom: _____, this day before God and these witnesses, with deepest joy, I receive you into my life to be one with you in marriage. As Christ is to the church, so by the grace of God, I will be to you—a loving and faithful husband, living my life for you, yet always exercising my headship over you even as Christ does over me. By the power of the Holy Spirit within me, I will fulfill all my responsibilities to you so that the love and righteousness of our Lord Jesus Christ might be manifested in our marriage.

Bride: _____, this day before God and these witnesses, I commit myself to you in marriage, knowing that God meant us for each other. I accept my responsibility to submit to you as the head of our household as a service to the Lord. By the power of the Holy Spirit within me, I will fulfill my obligations, realizing that our relationship is exclusive of all others and is permanent in the sight of God, and I will strive to become one person with you.

Selection 7

Groom: I, _____, take you, _____, to be my wedded wife;
And I do covenant and promise,
Before God and these witnesses to be your loving and faithful husband;
In plenty and in want; in joy and in sorrow;
In sickness and in health; as long as we both shall live.

Bride: I, _____take you, _____, to be my wedded husband;
And I do covenant and promise,
Before God and these witnesses to be your loving and faithful wife;
In plenty and in want; in joy and in sorrow;
In sickness and in health; as long as we both shall live.

Selection 8

Groom: I, _____, take thee, _____, to be my wedded wife, to have and to hold from this day forward, for better, for worse, for richer, for poorer, in sickness and in health, to love and to cherish as long as we both shall live, according to God's holy ordinance, and thereto I pledge thee my love.

Bride: I, _____ take thee, _____, to be my wedded husband, to have and to hold from this day forward, for better, for worse, for richer, for poorer, in sickness and in health, to love and to cherish as long as we both shall live, according to God's holy ordinance, and thereto I give thee my love.

Selection 9

Groom: I, _____, take you, _____, to be my wedded wife. With deepest joy I receive you into my life, that together we may be one. As Christ is to the church, so I will be to you—a loyal, sacrificial husband always performing my headship over you, even as Christ does over me. I promise you my deepest love and tender care. No matter where the Lord may lead us, I pledge you my life, as a loving and faithful husband.

Bride: I, _____, take you, _____, to be my wedded husband. With deepest joy I enter my new life with you. As is the church in her relationship to Christ, so I will be to you. I submit myself to your headship as to the Lord. I will live for you, loving you, learning from you, and seeking to please you. I pledge you my life as a loving, obedient, and faithful wife.

(Optional)
That like Ruth, I may say, "Whither thou goest, I will go; where thou lodgest, I will lodge; thy people shall be my people; and thy God, my God."

Selection 10

Groom: _____, this day before God as our witness, and these friends, I receive you into my life to be one with you in marriage.

As Christ loves the church and gave Himself for her, so I give myself for you to be a loving, faithful, and godly husband.

As Christ is head of the church and is responsible for her, so this day, by the grace of God, I assume full responsibility for you not only materially, but also physically, emotionally, and spiritually.

You are the most important person in my life next to the living Christ. I count you as a gift from God and as an answer to prayer. I will rely totally and completely on the work of the Holy Spirit in our lives to ensure that the Lord Jesus Christ is manifested in our marriage.

Bride: _____, this day before God and these witnesses I take you to be my husband, and I give to you all that I am and have.

I regard you as an answer to my prayers. You are the one God has chosen for me to complete. I submit myself to your headship as unto the Lord. Through the power and grace of Jesus Christ, I promise to love you with all of my being, to honor, respect, and esteem you above all others. I will comfort and care for you, endeavoring always to encourage and edify you. As we are blessed of God with children, I will strive to bring them up in the love and wisdom of God. As Jesus Christ is the most important person in our lives because He gave us life, I will seek to help you attain the stature and fullness of Christ as we serve Him together.

Appendix B: Ring Vows

Selection 1

Officiant: Now in God's sacred providence with us He has given us reminding tokens, and following this precedence you have chosen rings. These rings are of the most precious metal, which suggests the most priceless relationship on earth, that of a Christian home. Furthermore, the ring is endless until it is broken by an outside force, which fittingly represents the permanency of the marriage union until it's broken by the outside force of death. _____, in placing this ring, will you repeat after me these words.

Groom: I, _____, give you this ring, _____, as a token of my love, and I pledge you my loyalty and devotion until death separates us.

Officiant: _____, will you likewise, in placing this ring, repeat after me these words.

Bride: I, _____, give you this ring, _____, as a token of my love and I pledge you my loyalty and devotion until death shall separate us.

Section 2

Groom: _____, as a symbol of our new relationship with Christ and each other, I give you this ring, that you may wear it until the Father calls either of us to heaven.

Bride: _____, as a symbol of our new relationship with Christ and each other I give you this ring, that you may wear it until death separates us.

Selection 3

Groom: _____, as God has demonstrated throughout history His relationship with man giving a token as a sign of His covenant with man, so I too give you this ring as a token of my new relationship with you.

Bride: _____, just as Christ gave to us the bread and the wine to confirm His new covenant with us, so I give to you this ring to confirm our new covenant. Wear this ring, _____, as long as we both shall live in remembrance of our new relationship with one another.

Selection 4

Groom: _____, with this ring I proclaim that you are my wife, and I will call you Mrs. _____ for all the days of our life, or until our Lord returns.

Bride: _____, with this ring I call you my husband for all the days of our life, or until our Lord returns.

Selection 5

Officiant: What token do you give as an everlasting symbol of your love, sincerity, and faithfulness?

Groom: "A ring."

Officiant: As a ceaseless reminder of this hour and of the vow you have taken, place this ring, the symbol of your love, on the hand of your bride and repeat after me:

Groom: "With this ring I thee wed, with loyal love I thee endow, and all my worldly goods with thee I share, in the name of the Father, the Son, and Holy Spirit. Amen."

Officiant: What token do you give as an everlasting symbol of your love, sincerity, faithfulness and submission?

Bride: "A ring."

Officiant: As a ceaseless reminder of this hour and of the vow you have taken, place this ring, the symbol of your love, on the hand of your groom and repeat after me:

Bride: "With this ring I thee wed, with loyal love I thee endow, and all my wordly goods with thee I share, in the name of the Father, the Son, and Holy Spirit. Amen."

Appendix C: Unity Candle

Selection 1

For this cause a man shall leave his father and his mother, and shall cleave to his wife; and they shall become one flesh (Gen. 2:24).

Selection 2

The two outside candles of the center candelabra (have been lighted by the mothers to) represent the families and/or the lives of _____ and _____ to this moment. They are two distinct lights: each capable of going their separate ways. To bring bliss and happiness to their home, there must be the merging of these two lights into one light. This is what the Lord meant when He said, "On this account, a man shall leave his father and mother and be joined to his wife; and the two shall be one flesh." From now on their thoughts shall be one for each other, rather than for their own individual selves. Their joys and sorrows shall be shared alike. *As they each take* a candle and together light the center one, they will extinguish their own candle, thus letting the center represent the union of their lives into the one flesh. As this one light cannot be divided, neither shall their lives be divided, but be a united testimony to their unity in the Lord Jesus Christ.

Appendix D: "Reaffirming Family Ties"

In his attempt to include some acknowledgment of family ties, which is both relevant and significant, Pastor Edwin R. Lincoln suggests we rename the traditional "Giving Away of the Bride" and call it "Reaffirming Family Ties." He explains:

The parents of the groom and the mother of the bride are led to their seats in the traditional manner. The father escorts the bride down the aisle. But when she gets to where the groom is waiting, her father immediately sits with his wife.

At the point in the ceremony where the bride is normally given in marriage, I ask both sets of parents to come forward and stand behind their son and daughter. This follows:

"Mr. and Mrs. _____; Mr. and Mrs. _____; I have asked you to come forward now because your presence at this time is a rich testimony of the importance of family ties. You have encouraged _____ and _____ to come to this moment in the spirit of creating a new family constellation. You are giving your children to life's adventure, and not merely away from yourselves.

"This is what you raise your children for; to let them go—their way. And in their going, they come back again and again to share their discoveries and their joys with you. They confirm for you, who are parents, that you have fulfilled your task. Now, your new role is to support and encourage your son and daughter in theirs.

"It seems right, then, to ask you all, mothers and fathers, to make a vow, just as _____ and _____ will make theirs to each other in a moment.

"Do you support _____ and _____ in their choice of each other, and will you encourage them to build a home marked by openness, understanding, and mutual sharing? (The parents will answer, 'We do.') Mr. and Mrs. _____ and Mr. and Mrs. _____; thank you for your good influence and steady ways that bring _____ and _____ to this day."[1]

Notes

[1]Edwin R. Lincoln, "Reaffirming Your Family Ties," *Christianity Today*, Vol. XXIII, No. 8 (Jan. 19, 1979), pp. 32–33.